MASERATI

THE ROAD CARS

1981–1997

Other Titles in the Crowood AutoClassics Series

AC Cobra	Brian Laban
Alfa Romeo Spider	John Tipler
Alfa Romeo Sports Coupés	Graham Robson
Aston Martin DB4, DB5 and DB6	Jonathan Wood
Aston Martin DB7	Andrew Noakes
Audi quattro	Laurence Meredith
Audi TT	James Ruppert
Austin-Healey 100 & 3000 Series	Graham Robson
BMW 3 Series	James Taylor
BMW 5 Series	James Taylor
BMW Alpina	James Taylor
BMW M Series	Alan Henry
BMW: The Classic Cars of the 1960s and 70s	Laurence Meredith
BMW Z Series	Mick Walker
Citroën 2CV	Matt White
Citroën DS	Jon Pressnell
Cosworth and Ford	Graham Robson
Ferrari Dino	Anthony Curtis
Ford RS Escorts	Graham Robson
Imp	George Mowat-Brown
Jaguar E-Type	Jonathan Wood
Jaguar Mk 1 and 2	James Taylor
Jaguar XJ-S	Graham Robson
Jensen Interceptor	John Tipler
Jowett Javelin and Jupiter	Edmund Nankivell and Geoff McAuley
Lamborghini Countach	Peter Dron
Lancia integrale	Peter Collins
Lancia Sporting Coupés	Brian Long
Land Rover – Series One to Freelander	Graham Robson
Lotus and Caterham Seven: Racers for the Road	John Tipler
Lotus Elise	John Tipler
Lotus Esprit	Jeremy Walton
Mercedes-Benz Saloons: The Classic Models of the 1960s and 1970s	Laurence Meredith
Mercedes SL Series	Andrew Noakes
MGA	David G Styles
MGB	Brian Laban
MG T-Series	Graham Robson
Morgan Three-wheeler	Peter Miller
Porsche 911	David Vivian
Porsche Boxster	Gavin Farmer
Range Rover – The First Generation	James Taylor and Nick Dimbleby
Range Rover – The Second Generation	James Taylor
Riley – The Legendary RMs	John Price Williams
Rover P5 & P5B	James Taylor
Rover SD1	Karen Pender
Saab 99 and 900	Lance Cole
Sunbeam Alpine and Tiger	Graham Robson
Triumph Spitfire & GT6	James Taylor
TVR	John Tipler
Volkswagen Transporter	Laurence Meredith
Volvo 1800	David G Styles

MASERATI
THE ROAD CARS
1981–1997

John Price Williams

THE CROWOOD PRESS

First published in 2007 by
The Crowood Press Ltd
Ramsbury, Marlborough
Wiltshire SN8 2HR

www.crowood.com

British Library Cataloguing-in-Publication Data
A catalogue record for this book is available from the British Library.

ISBN 978 1 86126 890 7

Typeface used: Bembo.

Typeset and designed by D & N Publishing
Lambourn Woodlands, Hungerford, Berkshire.

Printed and bound in Singapore by Craft Print International.

Contents

Introduction 6
Acknowledgements 8

1 The saviour of Maserati 9
2 Launching the Biturbo 17
3 The Biturbo's mechanics 27
4 The 2.5 and intercooling 39
5 The first four-door cars – the 425 and 420 53
6 The Chryslerati – the Maserati TC 65
7 Major improvements – the 430 and 4.24v 75
8 The 228 81
9 The Spyder 89
10 The 222, its descendants and the four-valve engine 101
11 The Karif and its throbbing horses 115
12 The first Quattroportes and the V8 121
13 The V8 Shamal and the Fiat connection 127
14 The Ghibli 138
15 Fiat takes over and the Quattroporte IV 157
16 Buying and restoration – the Biturbo range 165

Useful contacts 173
Bibliography 175
Index 176

Introduction

The Biturbo era was a curious and fascinating time in the life of Maserati. It brought the company brought back from the brink of yet another imminent collapse, but in the eyes of many damaged the revered name of the Modena factory, which had produced beautiful and iconic cars from the 1930s to the 1970s.

The first Biturbos were woefully under-prepared to take to the road – sixteen years later the last Ghiblis lost a ton of money as Maserati sold them alongside the new 3200 coupé and its new owners, Ferrari, airbrushed away the De Tomaso years that had seen the birth of the Biturbo. The *New York Times* put it like this in October 2006:

> The ads said, 'The most exciting and totally new Maserati anyone can remember.' The Biturbo is now the Maserati that anyone who cares about the marque would like to forget.

Untrue and unfair. The bad odour engendered by the early models because of their unreliability has hung over the Biturbo like a cloud, even though the cars soon got better and better. Certainly they were still temperamental – so are Ferraris of that era – but they are fast, luxurious drivers' cars that reward the true enthusiast.

Today, the delightful Spyder, the civilized 430, the deliciously fast Ghibli Cup and all their Biturbo relatives are cherished as exceptional cars by those who acknowledge the quirks but appreciate the experience of owning and driving one. They are cars long overdue for reappraisal.

This book is about the Biturbo era – 1981 to 1998. Though the name itself disappeared in 1988, all the cars that followed it, excepting the Quattroporte, for the next ten years up to the 3200 coupé, were recognizably from the same Biturbo mould. As *Autocar* put it when they tested the last of the line, the Ghibli, '[it] is one more variation on the old Biturbo theme played by Maserati with ever-decreasing conviction'. (Despite this they loved it.)

And variations there were – at one time in the nineties there were eleven variants of the Biturbo on the home market in Italy. Confusing? Over a period of a few years there was the 222, the 222E, the 2.24v, the 222SE, the Racing, the 222SR, the 222.4v … even Maserati aficionados find themselves at sea on occasion. One magazine called it 'badge-engineering gone mad'. Not all models came to the UK – the total Biturbo production run was about 30,000 cars, of which some 700 reached Britain.

This book tries to make sense out of the Biturbo range and also covers the Quattroportes of the time; it goes into some detail on the 'Chrysler TC by Maserati' – a strange and often derided episode in Maserati history.

A note about the technical specifications. These can be a minefield, not only because of the plethora of models in production at the same time, and the chopping and changing of features on cars, but also because brochures and the documentation from the factory can be contradictory and imprecise. For instance, the literature on the Ghibli 2-litre, 2.8-litre and Cup maintains that they all weigh exactly 1,365kg, which is hardly likely given the changes in specification between them.

At one time there were catalysed and non-catalysed versions of models in production at the same time. The output figures given refer to non-catalysed engines, until catalysers became compulsory in Europe in 1993. Cars for the US market were always fitted with catalysers. Performance figures, except as specified otherwise, are factory figures, which are usually generous in their interpretation.

Acknowledgements

Journalists who write about cars will never know half as much as those who devote their lives to a particular marque, so first thanks must go to Andy Heywood at Bill McGrath Maserati, an acknowledged expert on all things related to the Tridente. Sitting above his busy workshop, he patiently briefed me on the intricacies of the model range between 1982 and 1998 and most importantly corrected me when I strayed into error, which in matters Maserati is deceptively easy. This book would not have been possible without his unstinting aid.

There was a legion of others who helped. Many members of the friendly and efficient Maserati Club UK talked about the history of their cars and allowed me to take pictures; in particular I would like to thank the club's administrator, Dave Smith, and the keeper of its archives, Adam Painter.

Thanks also to the brethren of that exclusive order, the Ghibli Cup drivers – Scot Crane, Henry McNeill and Duncan Mitchell – and to John Duggleby for talking about his Spyder.

First-hand recollections of the De Tomaso era came from Anthony Cazalet, Giordano Casarini and Luigi Maraffi. Robert Edmiston kindly gave me his recollections of trying to import the Biturbo into the UK.

In the USA, Karleen Tarola and Dr David George Briant of TC America Inc., the club for the Chrysler TC, helped with details of this rare beast and its Maserati connections; the pictures are the copyright of the Daimler-Chrysler Corporation and used with their permission.

Many pictures came from proud owners – Stephen Clahr, Matthew Leake, Nicholas Colquhoun-Denvers, Mike Roberts and David McCalium in the UK, Janpiet van der Weele in the Netherlands, Dan McCallum in Canada and Claus Müller in Germany. Every effort has been made to trace copyright holders of other pictures.

Jacopo Gessa of the Ferrari Maserati Image Service in Modena negotiated the use of some brochure pictures from Fonte Archivio Maserati. Thanks also to Silvia Pini of Maserati.

Enrico and his wonderful web pages, www.maserati-indy.co.uk/alfieri00a.htm, were most helpful.

Thanks to all of them; any errors are mine rather than theirs.

John Price Williams

1 The saviour of Maserati

The serious energy crisis and economic disarray of the 1970s led to grim times for the makers of fast, luxurious sports cars, particularly European specialists using thirsty, big-block American V8 engines in hand-built bodies. Down went Jensen in England, Monteverdi in Switzerland, Facel Vega in France, and in Italy both Iso and Bizzarrini.

Maserati was equally vulnerable: it was abandoned and put into bankruptcy on 23 May 1975 by its owner Citroën, who had bought it in 1968 for its engine and grand tourer expertise. As *Car* magazine put it, 'The French brought in a lot of men in suits who never got to grips with the Italian way of doing things and were finally defeated by economic Armageddon.'

Citroën had forced the development of a new V6 Maserati engine, which was then exported to France to be installed in Citroën's complex SM sports tourer, launched in March 1970. At Modena, the new engine was put to good use in the new and the successful Merak coupé. Sales of the SM were initially good but began tailing off in 1973, which had been a record year for Maserati in terms of cars produced – 738 cars, 430 of them Meraks – but escalating fuel prices and the adoption of lower speed limits in many countries hit not only SM production, but also Maserati's traditional markets, very hard.

Citroën was in parlous financial straits and could no longer absorb Maserati's losses. After straight-laced Peugeot took over eccentric Citroën in 1974, there was no room for such Italian indulgence, as the Maserati V6 was no longer of any use to the new group – they had a V6 of their own. Peugeot had already joined Volvo and Renault in a V6 engine-building venture called the Compagnie Française de Méchanique, based at Douvrin, near Lens in northern France. It had been set up to produce V8 engines, but downscaled to a V6 very similar to the Maserati equivalent during the fuel crisis.

There was uproar in Modena when Citroën pulled out. The local authority pledged to do all it could to save the plant, there was a workers' blockade, then finally the government coughed up enough cash to keep things ticking over for six months.

A saviour appears

Then ... *miraculoso* ... a saviour appeared just when it seemed the Maserati name was about to disappear. In November 1975, the flamboyant entrepreneur Alejandro De Tomaso, who made his own supercars such as the Pantera and Mangusta in Modena, announced that he was taking charge of Maserati, through his Benelli motorcycle interests.

De Tomaso liked doing things in style: the announcement was made with great show in the CanalGrande Hotel in Modena, which he both owned and lived in. He had a small office there, above the bar, in addition to his main office at the De Tomaso works in Modena.

He was, however, inheriting a nightmare. Industrial relations at the Viale Ciro Menotti factory in Modena were chaotic: more than half the year was lost in labour disputes with the 800 employees. Losses for 1974 amounted to the equivalent of £2.5 million. Production of 735 cars in 1973 had declined by 1975 to 201 cars, half of them Meraks, and in 1976 it fell to eighty-nine. Something had to be done. Ferrari, by contrast, produced more than a thousand cars in each of those years.

But it was not just the workers' fault: 1975 was the year of the deepest recession in Italy since the early 1950s and industrial output fell by almost 10 per cent.

It is said that De Tomaso paid 90,000 lira (£64) for control of the company in 1975, but 'control' was a flexible term: he ran the factory, but at that time had only 30 per cent of the equity as the majority was taken by the Italian government, which had intervened to save the company through its development agency, GEPI. Officially, GEPI took 70 per cent of the equity but offered De Tomaso – who, it was said, pretended reluctance – the option to buy it from them over six years for a total of about £4 million.

So Maserati was added to the clutch of Italian motor and motor-cycle industries under De Tomaso's control – even though he had sold Ghia and Vignale to Ford, he still owned Benelli, Moto Guzzi and Innocenti, most of these acquisitions funded by a benevolent GEPI, which supported him because he seemed to be able to bring some sort of stability to the anarchic labour relations in the industry.

The Innocenti acquisition from British Leyland in 1975 was particularly important, since it gave De Tomaso a considerable car production capacity in Milan, which was dedicated for the next few years to turning out versions of the Mini with BL engines and later with Daihatsu two- and three-cylinder engines. Innocenti could turn out 400 Mini-based cars a day, but production was usually half that figure, so there was a great deal of capacity available to build what De Tomaso wanted – a new, small, powerful Maserati that could compete with the likes of BMW, the car that was to become the Biturbo.

Back in Modena in 1975, De Tomaso had parlayed the working capital for Maserati out of £3.5 million handed out by Citroën to pay their debts as they fled back to France. The work now began to restructure the company, which was still highly labour- intensive.

Maseratis were still hand-built cars. The frame was made in the factory, the body panels arrived from the multitude of specialist *carrozzeria* around Turin and the castings for the engine came from a local foundry. Every engine was assembled by one man, then run on a test bed – the V6 for five hours and the V8 for seven. After that the sumps were removed and the bearings checked. Finally, the completed car was test-driven for 120 miles (195km).

It was obvious that the company would not survive with laborious methods and tiny sales volumes. In addition, during the 1970s, the performance of upmarket saloons such as the BMW had improved so much that the market for supercars was diminishing. New models and mechanisation had to be brought in, but this would take time.

The ten-year plan

De Tomaso had a ten-year plan – to produce high-performance, understated luxury cars at a price well below the Maserati sales tickets of the past. The key was mechanization and a smaller workforce. He recalled in an interview in 1983 that at the height of the Citroën ownership, there were more than 1,000 workers; when he took over Maserati there were 620 and, by the time the Biturbo began production, the figure at the Modena factory was down to 289. This was, of course, misleading since Modena was not then producing complete Biturbos, but supplying mechanical parts to Innocenti in Milan.

In the meantime, to freshen the product line, Maserati brought out in 1976 the Kyalami, a two-door coupé, which was not a new car but a lightly restyled version by Frua of the De Tomaso Longchamps, though it did have the four-camshaft Maserati V8 engine of 4,136cc instead of the Ford Cleveland of 5,763cc. Nearly 200 were built, which helped to keep the factory ticking over.

The father of the Biturbo – Alejandro De Tomaso

Alejandro De Tomaso – posing as a captain of Italian industry. He was one of the five owners Maserati has had in its nine decades of building cars. His achievement was to rescue the company with government aid when supercar makers were disappearing into financial oblivion.

Alejandro De Tomaso was a genius or a monster in the recollection of those who knew him. He may have been a combination of the two, but he was certainly a remarkable, far-seeing industrialist, who saved Maserati and for a time changed the face of the Italian car and motor cycle industry.

Someone who knew him closely is Giordano Casarini, former technical director of Maserati, who ran the experimental department, dynamometer rooms and the homologation process. He says of him: '[He was] the most intelligent person I have ever met, but he had a super-ego.'

De Tomaso was born in Argentina in 1928 to a landed family of Italian extraction, but fled to Italy in his twenties after falling out with the Peron régime. After the downfall of Peron he was able to return in 1956 to race a Maserati 150S in the Buenos Aires 1,000km race, in which he came fifth overall with Carlos Tomasi. It was the luckiest race he ever ran, because it was there that he met the wealthy Elizabeth (Isabelle) Haskell, a blonde from Red Bank, New Jersey, whose grandfather was one of the founders of General Motors.

In the following year's race, they partnered each other in a 1.5-litre Osca – the car built by the Maserati brothers after they had severed their relationship with the firm that bore their name and for whom De Tomaso worked as a test driver. They came sixth overall, and married shortly afterwards.

It was the financial backing from his wife's family and his own entrepreneurial skills that made De Tomaso an industrial titan in Italy in the 1970s and 1980s. He began in a modest way in 1959, founding his own company at Albareto, a suburb of Modena, firstly to turn out racing cars, then from 1963 exotic road cars such as the Vallelunga, Mangusta, Deauville, Pantera and Longchamp. They were characteristically Ford-engined with a central backbone chassis, and were not always V8 gas guzzlers. The Vallelunga, the world's first mid-engined, mass-produced sports car, had a 1500cc Ford Kent engine and a Volkswagen gearbox.

De Tomaso then picked up coachbuilders Ghia (while the owner was in jail), becoming its president in 1967, and then Vignale in 1969; the money for these acquisitions came mainly from his wife's family firm, Rowan Industries, who made electrical components in New Jersey.

He sold both coachbuilders to Ford in the 1970s for $2.8m, but there was a clause in the contract that forbade him from working for a competitor in the motor industry for the next five years, which is why he then turned his attention to motor cycles. However, the clause did not affect his own small-scale production in Modena of his own De Tomaso Automobili cars such as the Pantera.

De Tomaso specialized in waiting for companies to go bankrupt, then snapping them up with the help of lavish state aid. The vehicle for this was the government agency GEPI (Gestione e Participazione Industriale SpA), which used state cash to save workers' jobs in failing industries. State intervention was common throughout Europe in the 1970s; the British government had nationalized British Leyland the same year, but to no good effect.

GEPI was then run by Romano Prodi, a highly successful politician who was to become Italian prime minister – most recently in 2006 – and president of the European Commission. But even for Italy it was a curious organization: at one time it owned a bankrupt Italian shipyard and offered to give a free Maserati to anyone who bought one of its ships.

continued overleaf

The father of the Biturbo – Alejandro De Tomaso *continued*

In the early 1970s GEPI supported De Tomaso in his purchase of Italian motor cycle manufacturers Benelli, and then Moto Guzzi. By 1975 the Ford clause had expired so GEPI was able to help him buy Maserati that year and later Innocenti, who made among other things Lambretta scooters and a derivative of the British Leyland Mini.

This outpouring of cash was due to the close links that De Tomaso and other industrialists had to the ruling Christian Democrat party. They were, for instance, able to get the government to ban the import of motor cycles under 380cc (a huge benefit for scooter-maker De Tomaso) and to limit Japanese car imports to a thousand a year.

Apart from controlling most of Italy's motor cycle industry, De Tomaso was once the third largest car manufacturer in Italy after Fiat and state-owned Alfa Romeo. Once memorably described as 'Bonaparte in a blue business suit', he was a dynamic, flamboyant character, artful in seizing opportunity, of quick temper and decided views. 'Liked by the few, detested by the many', was one verdict.

A British engineer from GKN, who travelled to Modena regularly to deal with De Tomaso over the supply of differentials, recalled recently that he was one of the most frightening persons he had ever met.

Robert Edmiston, who fought a fruitless battle in the early 1980s to try to get him to produce right-hand-drive Biturbos recalled: 'He was a very, very difficult person, someone I could never get to know or like.'

Maserati UK's former technical director, Anthony Cazalet, recalls waiting for De Tomaso in the CanalGrande Hotel in Modena, which the tycoon owned and lived in. 'We would all sit about in the lobby then De Tomaso would arrive with a trail of terrified people behind him. He was very unpleasant; the only person he would not trample on was Aurelio Bertocchi, the chief engineer.'

There were constant battles within Maserati. Giordano Casarini recalls testing a Shamal on the Nardò track at up to 270km/h. De Tomaso was not satisfied, calling for more boost: 'We told him this could not be done, but he said 'F— the engineers, do as I say. We blew the engine.'

On another occasion he announced at a meeting that 'my guys' (his own De Tomaso engineers) had worked out that a Biturbo engine would do 20km on a litre of petrol. Casarini, who looked on them as good field mechanics rather than thermodynamics experts, protested that this was impossible and that the figure was half of this. 'De Tomaso asked me to leave the room. On the way back they broke down – they had run out of petrol.'

Despite the tantrums, he could be pragmatic, once defining his management style by saying to Casarini: 'If I take ten decisions today, two will be wrong – but eight will be right.'

De Tomaso could have been just another South American playboy – his own family wealth and the considerably larger fortune of his wife could have ensured that – but he was a driven man, working from early morning to late at night, who brooked no opposition and could fly into rages when questioned, some of them undoubtedly strategic, as he sought to bully suppliers.

George Garbutt, who ran the Maserati import operation in Baltimore and worked with him for many years, recalled his experiences in the excellent *iL Tridente* magazine of the US Maserati Club. He was a small, arrogant man. 'I have seen his secretary burst into tears when he was in a rage about something, but one-to-one he was a normal person.'

He was intensely superstitious and would always announce a new car on 14 December, the anniversary of the founding of Maserati, and would never make a major decision on a Tuesday. He always wore his wristwatch on top of the cuff of his shirt sleeve – an affectation probably copied from Gianni Agnelli of Fiat – and he invariably wore a yellow scarf, whatever the weather.

On his take-over of Maserati, the first major casualty, apart from hundreds of workers whose jobs GEPI had been trying to preserve, was the legendary chief engineer, Giulio Alfieri, who had been responsible for almost everything Maserati had produced since the mid-1950s. It was an act of revenge.

Dr Adolfo Orsi, grandson of the Orsi patriarch who ran Maserati from 1938, recalled that when they were about to sell the company to Citroën in 1968, De Tomaso had come in with an alterative offer which the Orsis were tempted to take, but they had been talked out of it by Alfieri. De Tomaso never forgave him and Dr Orsi maintained that the day after the company fell into De Tomaso's hands more than a decade later, Alfieri found his belongings in the car park when he came to work. According to Peter Pijlman in his book on the [Citroën] SM, *De Diva*, Alfieri left behind in the car park his own SM, in which he had installed a Maserati V8. He went uttering threats of legal action. 'We disagreed on almost everything', he said later. (He became technical director of Lamborghini and designed the quattrovalvole cylinder head for the Countach.)

Then there was the 1982 Falklands war, which, being Argentinian, De Tomaso would have called *La guerra de las Malvinas*. But far from standing by his native country, he announced that he was renouncing his citizenship in disgust at their surrender to Margaret Thatcher's government.

The British journalist Tony Dron neatly summed up the enigma of De Tomaso, who was wont to promise much, in a 1983 interview after the launch of the Biturbo: 'When he states blandly that Maserati production this year will be about 6,400 cars, I don't know whether to believe him implicitly or divide by four.' (In fact De Tomaso was not far wrong: production that year was 6,180.)

He eventually fell out with his partner, the American importer Kjell Qvale. 'The Biturbo was a lively, attractive car', Qvale wrote in his autobiography. 'Sales were good and we were financially successful. Unfortunately there was one particular problem with the car that resulted in a specific part needing replacement. It took us a long time to get De Tomaso to agree to produce a replacement.'

Qvale had threatened to stop importing Maseratis unless this unspecified problem was fixed and when sometime later his general manager was visiting the factory De Tomaso told him that the design of the cars was up to him, De Tomaso, and if Kvale did not like it he could quit. End of partnership. 'Our friendship suffered considerably,' wrote Kvale, 'and it was many years before we got together again.'

In the late 1980s and 1990s the empire diminished: Maserati and Innocenti fell into the hands of Fiat, Moto Guzzi went to Finprogetti and Benelli to Merloni. The De Tomaso Automobili factory in Modena remained Italy's only independent car manufacturer, but it was not to last. One tale tells of De Tomaso's wife, who used to ride a Benelli six-cylinder motor cycle to the plant, disconsolately picking weeds in the garden in front of the factory.

De Tomaso had a serious stroke in January 2003 and spent the last few months of his life in a wheelchair. He died in May that year at the age of sixty-four. A funeral chapel was set up in the De Tomaso works in Modena and the funeral took place on 21 May at the church of San Pietro, near his CanalGrande Hotel. There was one black Ghibli Cup parked nearby.

In November 1999 the Mangusta appeared again as a 2+2 Ford V8-engined sports car, based on a De Tomaso prototype, the Bigua, and renamed the Kvale Mangusta.

It was built by De Tomaso's old American friends, the Qvale Automotive Group, who bought a factory in Modena and installed Giordano Casarini as managing director. The project ran into financial difficulties and after production of 284 cars, the factory was closed.

Shortly afterwards the project was bought by MG Rover and the car redesigned as the MG XPower Sport Veloce, with which Casarini has been closely associated.

The final production car to bear De Tomaso's name was the Guarà, which had first appeared at the Geneva motor show in 1993 and whose body was said to be based on the Maserati Barchetta Stradale prototype. It had a mid-mounted 4.6-litre Ford V8. A V8 by BMW of four litres was offered earlier. About fifty were made before the plant closed.

De Tomaso's son, Santiago, continues to promote his father's remarkable achievements.

One of the first Biturbos, used for road tests. It was the car driven by Motor *in the spring of 1983. The testers were told that though the lines were strongly influenced by Giugiaro, it was De Tomaso himself who had drawn them up. They 'avidly hoped' that the car would reach the UK very soon, but it was to be more than three and a half years before it did so. (LAT)*

Early cars were offered with two steering rack ratios; the test car had the slower one and was thought to be rather low-geared. Customers were dissuaded from asking for power steering, probably because it was too much trouble at a time when the factory was ramping up production. (LAT)

The first hint of what was to become the Biturbo came in late 1976 from the general manager and managing director at the Viale Ciro Menotti factory, Aurelio Bertocchi, son of the famous Maserati test driver and chief mechanic Guarino Bertocchi (often misspelt Guerino), who had been with Maserati since the Targa Florio of 1926.* When a party of British journalists visited the factory, he told them that a new car with a completely new engine was being planned. It was to be a two-litre 2+2 with a four-valve engine. It had yet to be styled, but was scheduled for production in the spring of 1978. Optimism indeed, though there had been a Giugiaro 2+2 styling exercise, which appeared on an Indy chassis at the Turin show in 1974.

Appeal to the young

The way Bertocchi told it, the new car would appeal to the younger man (sic) not concerned with tradition, who wanted an easily serviceable machine. The larger Maseratis were for the older man, who remembered the famous cars of the past and could afford to service and look after their more highly tuned engines.

He also made it clear that Citroën suspension and braking systems would find no place in the new car. De Tomaso, he said, wanted to fit 'good, ordinary, reliable British brakes to all Maseratis'. He had particular scorn for the Citroën-based Quattroporte, still being made in tiny numbers only for the Middle East and South America, which had not been submitted for European testing: it was too heavy, had too little power and the suspension was too complicated.

So plans were being made for the transformation of Maserati and the first, heavily disguised prototypes of the new coupé could be seen undergoing trials on the outskirts of Modena during early 1980. De Tomaso was able to announce the coming of the Biturbo at the Turin motor show in April 1980, and a picture of a camouflaged version appeared the following month. But bringing the plans to fruition was to take much longer than expected.

The Biturbo was a startling change of direction for a company whose name had been made manufacturing hand-built, large-engined supercars. It was a series production car, with

*Guarino was to be killed in the passenger seat of a De Tomaso Deauville on the *autostrada* on 13 April 1981. Aurelio died in the passenger seat of an Innocenti prototype, which crashed into a truck.

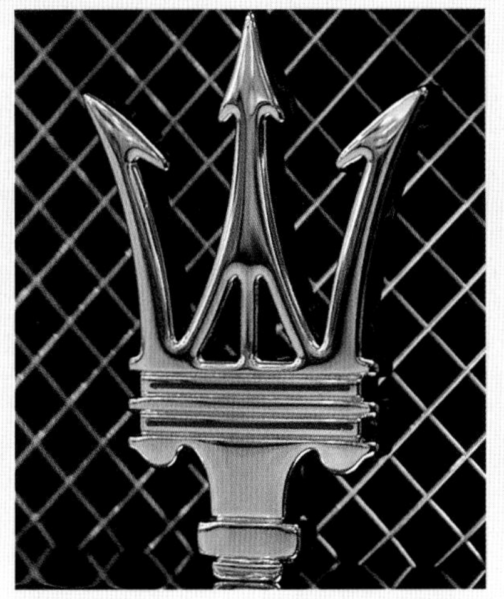

Il Tridente

The famous trident symbol that has characterized the Maserati marque was based on the statue of Neptune, aka Poseidon, who holds his trident in his right hand as he overlooks in rather camp fashion the Piazza Maggiore, the city square of Bologna, whose inhabitants call him 'the giant'.

The three-pronged spear is the symbol of the authority of Neptune as the classical god of waters, seas and storms. It is as closely associated with Maserati as Ferrari is with its prancing horse; some even referring archly to the firm as casa del Tridente.

Il Tridente was first used in an oblong shape on the radiator of the Maserati brothers' first complete car, a 1500cc supercharged straight eight, the tipo 26. The emblem is thought to have been designed by the seventh Maserati brother, Mario, a painter, who played no part in the motor business.

It has since gone though many stylized forms on Maserati grilles, boots, wheels, filler caps, steering wheels, pedals and anywhere else a logo could be stuck, including being embossed into leather headrests. On the 425, for instance, it could be found on the grille, boot, door handles, fuel cap lid, door kick plates, clock, dashboard, wheels, plenum chamber and steering wheel.

The Neptune fountain was the first to be built in renaissance Europe, in 1566, and is the work of a Flemish sculptor Jean Boulogne de Douai, known in the city as Il Fiammingo or Giambologna – 'little John of Bologna'. It has undergone several indignities. At one stage Napoleon replaced it with a statue of himself and in the time of papal states, scandalized women were protected from the sight of Neptune's not inconsiderable privates by a pair of bronze trousers (now removed). Giambologna's masterpiece, Flying Mercury, is in the Bargello, Florence.

pressed steel rather than hand-crafted panels, designed to sell widely in the mid-range BMW/Alfa Romeo and Mercedes sector, and more importantly to make money, something Maserati had been largely unsuccessful at doing over many years.

At the time it was announced, Maserati were building around three cars a day – two Quattroportes and one of the other three cars left in the range, a Merak, Kyalami or Khamsin.

Production for 1981 was 555 cars and De Tomaso's plan was to increase this dramatically – figures of 7,000–10,000 cars a year were mentioned, based largely on assumed demand and the predicated production capacity of the new lines at the Innocenti works in Milan, which were to assemble the car.

Government loans

Huge amounts of money, largely soft loans from the Italian government, had been pumped into the Biturbo project to make the wheels turn. New facilities, like an extensively automated body and paint plant, with anti-corrosion dipping, had been constructed at Innocenti's Lambrate plant, which took on another 200 workers. In Modena, a new production line employing 150 at the Viale Ciro Menotti factory had been put in at a cost of some £20m, to manufacture engines and suspension units, which were then sent to Milan to be assembled into the body.*

Much was made at the time of the anti-corrosion dips at Lambrate, but it was to transpire that all was not well. Early cars were to suffer

*The exceptions were the Spyder and some of the later cars like the Karif, which were built at Modena. When the Innocenti works at Lambrate closed in 1993 all production was transferred there.

corrosion, which suggested that rusty panels had been used in the build.

The Biturbo was quite unlike anything else on the road: it was the first series-production car with a twin turbocharged engine, the small Japanese turbos being directly related to those developed for Moto Guzzi motorcycles in another part of De Tomaso's empire.

Turbocharging, he announced presciently at the launch, was the way of the future and would appear on more and more fast touring cars. Indeed, by 1999, IHI (Ishikawajima-Harima Heavy Industries Co. of Japan), the shipbuilding and engineering conglomerate that made the Maserati turbos, had delivered eight million to the automotive industry worldwide.

Several car manufacturers now use twin turbos, but the name itself has been revived by the Alpina D10 Biturbo, an expensive modification of the BMW 530D put together in Germany by Burkhard Bovensiepen. It has twin Garrett T25 turbochargers arranged in parallel, which is said to remove almost all turbo lag.

The Biturbo was the world's first series production car with a twin-turbocharged engine, and looked completely different from its competitors.

Alpina claims a 0–100km/h (0–62mph) time of 6.8sec and a top speed of 158mph (245km/h), making it the fastest diesel saloon in the world at the time of writing.

No wonder Maserati were swamped with orders after the Biturbo's unveiling in Italy. It was a supercar priced at not much more than an ordinary car. Prices were to rise steeply before it made it into the showrooms. (Fonte Archivio Maserati)

2 Launching the Biturbo

The car that saved Maserati – new, fast, luxurious and initially cheap – was introduced to the press by a beaming De Tomaso on 14 December 1981 – the 67th anniversary of the founding of the Societa Anonima Officine Alfieri Maserati in Pontevecchio, Bologna. That day had also been a Monday and the superstitious De Tomaso was to make a habit of announcing new cars on 14 December.

The year 1981 had been a relatively good year for Maserati: the factory had produced 528 cars, nearly 400 of them Quattroportes, but production of Meraks, Kyalamis and Khamsins was being wound down to make way for the new wonder car that would transform the firm's fortunes. As De Tomaso put it, 'The car has such outstanding qualities and such a competitive price that it really is a first step in a serious effort for the industrial development of Maserati.'

There were those who thought that Maserati was making a serious mistake by abandoning its sports car heritage. They pointed out that Lamborghini had made a huge success of the Countach, rather ignoring the fact that Lamborghini had itself slid into bankruptcy in 1980 before being rescued by two French food tycoons. Running a sports car company is a high-wire act at the best of times, whose dangers are not confined to the Italian motor industry: Aston Martin in England has been insolvent seven times and has produced cars in five different locations.

But it was not the best of times to launch any new car in Italy: the start of 1982, for instance, saw state-controlled Alfa Romeo, hit by a slump in demand, shutting down production lines for months and laying off 14,000 workers out of its staggering total of 43,000 employees. Alfa, like Maserati, was a company well used to facing financial disaster and like its Modena counterpart had been bailed out by the state, but very much earlier. (In 1934 Alfa was taken over by an agency of Mussolini's Fascist government, the Instituto di Riconstruzzione Industriale, which controlled it for more than half a century until Fiat took over in 1987.)

Despite the gloom in the rest of the Italian motor industry, De Tomaso maintained his usual ebullience and it seemed justified, as after the Italian papers had reported the launch just before Christmas, 236 orders arrived within five days. Between Christmas and New Year another 100 were received. Potential buyers were so keen that thousands of people put down deposits on a car whose price had yet to be finally fixed, giving De Tomaso yet more capital to start building the car. As Antonello Cucchi put it in his book *New Maseratis*, 'The Italians went wild; it rained reservations, and strings were pulled in high places to try to jump the queue.'

Top speed of 133mph

Enthusiasm was stoked by the Italian magazine *AutoCapital*, which reported that the Biturbo was an extraordinarily good car for such a low price. It deserved huge praise and was unrivalled in the tax-saving two-litre class with its top speed of 215km/h (133mph). 'Time will reveal its defect and weak points', it declared presciently, 'but there is still no doubt that the Biturbo is a significant car that will spell trouble for its rivals.'

By the time of the Geneva motor show in March 1982, when the first deliveries for the Italian domestic market had been promised, a thousand cars had been sold – even though the Biturbo was nowhere near volume production. Soon these orders doubled.

The new car was to be sold in Italy for a tax-paid price of only £8,000, the cheapest Maserati ever built by far. It was about the same price as the two-litre Lancia Gamma saloon – and half the price in Italy of the Porsche 911 SC. The price turned out to be suspiciously low for a Maserati – after all, in the same year in Britain, the Merak SS was selling for the equivalent of £19,000, and the Kyalami and the Khamsin for between £26,000 and £29,000. (Conversions to sterling have been done as the contemporary Italian lira figures are fairly meaningless.)

De Tomaso, in his bullish launch speech, had promised production from March 1982 at the rate of about thirty cars a day, though the capacity was available to build 120. There would be a right-hand-drive version for the UK 'in a year or so', where the price would be around £10,000. Then there would be a model for the USA at the equivalent of £14,400 ($16,000).

Alas, these prices were to rocket before the Biturbo landed on the shores of Britain and America. There was obviously an element of underpricing when the car was introduced, but the continuing enemy over the decade was Italian inflation, which averaged 10 per cent – it was, for instance, four times the rate of that in Germany.

But it was no wonder that the factory was flooded with orders at the outset and it was not just the pricing: apart from the mechanical refinement and the esteemed Maserati *tridente* on the front grille, the specification was outstanding.

It was essentially a no-extras car, at a time when people like BMW were still charging extra for a radio, and unusually for the USA no options at all were available with the first American specification cars.

Luxury and warmth

The Biturbo had a four-speaker Mitsubishi stereo radio/cassette system and an impressive list of other standard equipment: light alloy wheels, air conditioning, central locking, electric windows and remote-control mirrors. The interior was decorated with a corduroy fabric, with a possible leather option, and the whole cabin gave an air of luxury and warmth. To allow passengers into the back, the front seats slid forward when the backs were folded. The steering wheel was adjustable for rake and height: useful for those who did not favour the traditional, crouched, Italian driving position.

The distinctive sharp edges and straight lines of the wedge-shape unit-construction body were designed at De Tomaso's own facilities, though many saw a likeness to the works of Giugiaro, particularly as the front-end was reminiscent of the Quattroporte. Most observers agreed that the coupé was wedge-shaped. Not so Maserati. A brochure for the Biturbo SE described it as 'quite unlike the "flying wedges" normally associated with Italian sports cars'.

Scale models were apparently tested in a wind tunnel, but not the full-size car, since De Tomaso apparently did not want to compromise its looks, relying on engine development and cutting down weight to achieve his ends. Proper crash testing, which had to be done, took place at the MIRA facility in England and endurance testing was done on the circular track at Nardò in southern Italy.

The car's stance on the road was more like that of a sports car than a saloon; squat and purposeful, it looked powerful and exciting, despite being a three-box, four-seat configuration. The effect was achieved partly because it was a two-door car with extensive stainless steel window surrounds, but it was also shorter than its peers: at 163.5in (413.5cm) it was a whole 14in (35.5cm) less than a BMW 320; it was wider by 4.1in (10.4cm) and lower by 2.9in (7.3cm). It weighed 2,395lb (1,086kg).

The body was not to everyone's taste: one American publication compared it to the greatly unloved Cadillac Cimarron, introduced at about the same time and based on the Chevrolet Cavalier. (The Cimarron was subsequently voted eighth worst car of the millennium by the website www.cartalk.com.) But the Biturbo suffered no such ignominy and its sharp lines were widely praised.

There was some evidence of cost cutting: the square front lights came from the Volkswagen Scirroco Mk 2 for the US version and the side lights from the Fiat 127 for the European cars. The early facias in the Biturbo's life cycle were not real wood, but could pass for it, and what looked like leather in some places was not from any animal.

Autocar was one of the first magazines to test the new car in Italy, in a very short drive at the Italian launch: 'The car leaps away impressively from rest, even before the turbos come into action, accompanied by the sporty sound of a high-efficiency engine at work up front.'

Prices in Italy rose before the first cars had been built: the launch figure of around £8,000 had become more than £9,000 by April 1982 and nearly £11,000 by June – with still nothing delivered. It was not until December 1982, a whole year after the launch, that the Biturbo started to become widely available. The delay had caused much sarcastic comment by Italian journalists, who were then colourfully derided by Maserati writer Antonello Cucchi as 'those who roost in dead trees like condors, ready to croak their envy to the winds'.

Turbo problems

One of the pre-production problems was with the turbos that had been ordered from IMI, who until now had made only aftermarket turbos. It was discovered that the attachment of the wastegate was faulty, so all the turbos were sent back to Japan for modification.

Production was said to be running at only thirty-five cars a month in early 1983, but it suddenly leapt ahead and by the end of the year 5,333 Biturbos had been built.

When *Motor* tested the one of the first production models in the spring of 1983 the Biturbo had gone up again to more than £12,000 in Italian prices. The testers were unable to drive it flat-out due to the notorious fog that can hang around Modena. (The local joke is that the city was spared in the swathe of devastation that Attila the Hun wreaked in northern Italy because he could not find Modena in the murk.)

The drivers squeezed 127mph (203km/h) out of the car, failing, because of the fog, to reach the claimed 133mph (214km/h) maximum, which they pointed out would be over the 6,300rpm red line. They revved to 6,600rpm in all the other gears, reaching 115mph (185km/h) in fourth and 83mph (134km/h) in third.

They seemed to have encountered no major faults, but these soon became apparent as more cars were delivered. Despite the time taken to get the Biturbo into production, testing had been hurried and a final rush to get the lines moving left many faults undiscovered; they emerged in the major market, the USA, as irritating problems at best and engine failures at worst.

Early cars, for instance, often dubbed the Biturbo I series, though this was never their official name, suffered from seized turbochargers, due to drivers not taking the handbook's advice to let the engine idle after a long run to cool the turbos. Then there were broken timing belts – sometimes due to enthusiastic over-revving. There was, however, a basic fault with the timing belt tensioner, which resulted in many bent valves and took three revisions to cure.

The litany of failures continued with overheating, melting fuse boxes, cracked wires in the distributor, oil leaks from the transmission and stuttering engines on left turns due to mis-set float levels in the carburettor, the ubiquitous Weber 36 DCNVH (the 36 is the diameter of the throttle butterfly). Giordano Casarini had a special float made by Weber to try to overcome this problem.

It didn't help that there were three slightly different versions of this carburettor fitted to the

2.5 at the same time. For the European market there was the DCNVH 18, for Switzerland the DCNVH 25 and for the USA the DCNVH 24, all jetted slightly differently. Another Weber, the 34DAT28, was fitted in 1986.

Hot-starting difficult

One of the perpetual faults, which still dogs early cars, was the refusal to start when the engine is hot. As the original carburettor did not have a fuel return, the petrol was pumped in and kept in check by the needle valve, so it got hot in the flow bowl, making starting difficult. Restarting up to ten minutes after switching the engine off is usually no problem, but the heat soak between ten minutes and an hour can make starting a lottery. There was a stream of service bulletins from the importers to dealers telling them, for instance, in the USA to maintain the carburettor float level at 43mm, in Switzerland at 42.5mm and in the rest of Europe at 44mm.

In hot American states, rubber door trims had to be treated with silicone to prevent sticking, which destroyed the seals, and the sun bleached the grey and black paint around the windows. The solution for this was to treat the area with rubbing compound and Armorall. Another rubber problem was with the early Pirelli tyres, which quickly acquired flat spots after becoming warm.

More serious in the very early cars, before UK imports began, were mechanical disasters due to premature wear in the timing belt tensioners. These were not fitted initially with a greasing nipple, and had to be removed for lubrication. A nipple was eventually fixed, but it was not mentioned in the maintenance schedule, so often went ungreased.

Camshafts on early cars were prone to seizing in their housing due to oil starvation, particularly on the left side as oil from the pump reached this side last. This led to very expensive warranty claims. There were at least four different oil pumps fitted during pre-production. Then there were rear axle problems caused by overheating – the breather hole was not large enough, and pressure built up, which damaged the oil seals.

The early dash was rectangular and rather clumsy. (Fonte Archivio Maserati)

It was soon replaced with the elliptical dash, which lasted virtually unchanged until the end of production.

More avoidable was the disintegration of turbos, caused by foreign objects getting into the inlet tracts. This usually happened after servicing when things such as sockets and clips were left in the air filter box and found their way into the piping. Maserati refused to pay any warranty claims for this failure after the first free 1,000-mile service, a ten-hour marathon.

Giordano Casarini, Maserati's technical director at the time, is clear where the blame lies for the early reliability problems: 'Lack of quality is due to lack of testing.' In the Biturbo's case, De Tomaso let the Italian public do his testing for him. It seems that his headlong rush in to production was unstoppable, even by his senior staff. 'We would have a fight a day', said Casarini, 'and if we backed him into a corner over something he would just answer "my right ball tells me to do it"'.

Another substantial part of the reason for the reliability issues was De Tomaso's continuing search for economies, which made him unwilling to change anything until all the factory stocks of the offending item had been used up, according to George Garbutt, who ran the American import operation and knew him well. This turned out in many cases to be a false economy, since delaying the changes meant increasing warranty costs, because labour then had to be factored in as well.

The Biturbo II

Not all of the design faults, particularly the melting fuse boxes – units which had originated in the Fiat Strada – were cured quickly, but many were overcome with the introduction of what the factory called the Biturbo II. Production began on 21 March 1985, without a break from the original model. A brochure in Italian heralded it as *le nuove generazioni* and it was perhaps what the Biturbo should have been on its introduction, though some aficionados still prefer the early models.

The reliability issues were addressed in several ways. Firstly the maze of piping under the bonnet became even more complex with the introduction of water cooling for the turbos, which Maserati claimed reduced their running temperatures to 320°F (160°C). If the car was switched off after a long run, a thermosyphon dealt with the heat soak and continued to cool the turbines. 'Such a technological improvement means full reliability of the engine, even after 60,000 miles and over, thanks to the constant and perfect run of the turbines' said the brochure. Nevertheless, today's advice is still to let the engine idle before switch-off to reduce turbine temperatures, as too-rapid cooling can be dangerous.

The water pump was redesigned with a 77mm impeller rather than 75mm and this modification was done from engine 103286. The clutch and timing belt tensioners were also redesigned, but more importantly a new device called the Maserati Automatic Boost Control (MABC) was fitted, which had also been on some earlier cars. This restricted the boost pressure when necessary and cut the ignition if the engine was over-revved. Until then, heavy-footed drivers were restrained by a limiter in the distributor and the sight of the boost gauge creeping into the red.

Essentially, the MABC was much the same as the APC system devised by Saab, which balanced the turbo boost according to the load on the engine and the quality of the fuel being used. In traditional turbos of the time, boost pressure was adjusted by allowing some of the gases to bypass the turbos and escape though wastegates opened by a diaphragm valve operated by the pressure of the compressor. In the

Fuel vaporization was a major problem in the early cars. One attempt at a solution was the tiny white pump seen here in front of the polished plenum chamber, which was meant to draw out heat and fumes from the overheating carburettor beneath. It was not a success.

Biturbo coupé/i/Si/S (1982–88)

Engine – coupé

Type	AM452/093
Layout	V6 90 degrees – 3 valves per cylinder, single overhead cam per bank, two IHI turbo-chargers
Bore × stroke:	82 × 63.5mm
Capacity:	1996cc
Compression ratio:	7.8:1
Max power:	180bhp/134.2kW@ 6,000rpm
Max torque:	186lb ft/25.8kg m@4,400rpm
Fuel system:	Weber twin-choke carburettor
Intercoolers:	None

Engine – coupé i As above except:

Type	AM470
Layout	V6 90 degrees – 3 valves per cylinder, single overhead cam per bank, two IHI turbo-chargers, fuel injection
Bore × stroke:	82 × 63.5mm
Capacity:	1996cc
Compression ratio:	7.8:1
Max power:	185bhp/136.2kW@6,000rpm
Max torque:	186lb ft/25.8kg m@4,400rpm

Engine – coupé Si As above except:

Type	AM471
Layout	V6 90 degrees – 3 valves per cylinder, single overhead cam per bank, two IHI turbo-chargers, fuel injection
Bore × stroke:	82 × 63.5mm
Capacity:	1996cc
Compression ratio:	7.8:1
Max power:	220bhp/161.3kW@6,000rpm
Max torque:	186.8lb ft/26kg m@3,500rpm

Engine – coupé S As above except:

Type	AM452.10
Layout	V6 90 degrees – 3 valves per cylinder, single overhead cam per bank, two IHI turbo-chargers, fuel injection
Bore × stroke:	82 × 63.5mm
Capacity:	1996cc
Compression ratio:	7.8:1
Max power:	205bhp/153kW@6,000rpm
Max torque:	172lb ft/23.9kg m@4,400rpm
Fuel system:	Weber twin-choke carburettor
Intercoolers:	Two

Transmission

Gearbox:	ZF manual 5 speed + reverse. Automatic three-speed option
Final drive:	Sensitork 3.73:1

Suspension

Front:	MacPherson strut with anti-roll bar, coil springs, shock absorbers
Rear:	Trailing arms, coil springs, shock absorbers, anti-roll bar
Steering:	Power-assisted rack and pinion
Brakes:	Servo-assisted twin circuit, front and rear ventilated discs with floating calipers, rear drum parking brake

Running gear

Wheels:	6J × 14
Tyres:	195/60VR 14 MXV

Performance

Max speed:	133mph (225km/h)
Acceleration:	0–62mph (100km/h) in 6.5sec

Dimensions

Wheelbase:	99in (2,514mm)
Front track:	55.9in (1,420mm)
Rear track:	56.3in (1,431mm)
Length:	163.5in (4,153mm)
Width:	67.5in (1,714mm)
Height:	51.4in (1,305mm)
Weight:	2,395lb (1,086kg)

Number built: *11,919*

The boost gauge

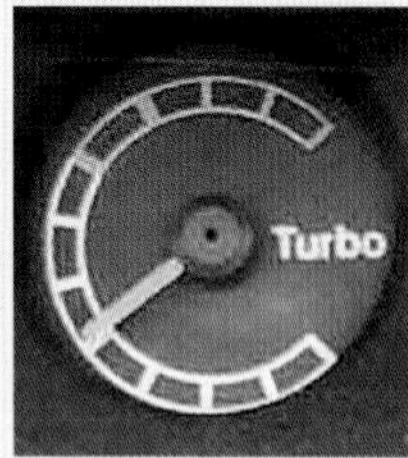

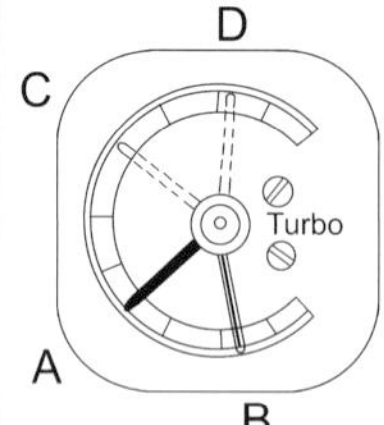

The boost gauge has annoyed hundreds of Biturbo drivers because of its imprecision and lack of calibration. It works by indicating the pressure in the intake manifold and thus the efficiency of the turbochargers. This was how it was explained to owners:

A Engine not running – pointer indicates the atmospheric pressure.
B Engine running at low speed or on overrun – vacuum effect takes place.
C Engine running normally as turbos create overpressure.
D Panic mode if pointer frequently goes into red area or stays there. Maserati advice was to slow down and have the car checked as soon as possible.

MABC, the boost pressure was adjusted by an electronic control unit.

Another advantage was that it prevented one of the drawbacks of turbocharging – forcing the mixture in too quickly, resulting in premature detonation causing 'knock', which can seriously damage a turbocharged engine. A knock sensor screwed into the middle V of the block was linked to the control unit to prevent this. Many turbo engines ran with low compression ratios to knock, but the MABC allowed not only a high compression ratio with protection from knock, but also cut out the ignition if the engine was over-revved.

The Nikasil coating on the cylinder liners had caused a problem because the chrome hardening fell off, so this was abandoned.

Because the GKN two-pin differential had difficulty handling the power of the Biturbo engine and caused a serious lack of grip on wet roads, it was replaced with a more sophisticated Sensitork limited-slip unit, sometimes known as the Torsen (short for torque-sensing). The name Sensitork seems to have been a De Tomaso marketing wheeze. The gears were manufactured by the Gleason Corporation and fitted into the GKN axle. If one rear wheel slipped or lifted off the ground, it could put up to 90 per cent of the power through the other. The earlier differentials had breather holes that were too small and easily became blocked, leading the axle to overheat and destroy oil seals. In some of the early cars the differentials went within two years.

The Biturbo II was a big improvement on the original model, which had been put into production with inadequate testing. (Fonte Archivio Maserati)

Interior improvements

There were also improvements to the interior. The boxy, rectangular, 1970s-looking dash was replaced by a much better semi-circular unit and the digital quartz clock between the air vents disappeared to be replaced, for the first time in a Biturbo, by the gold Lasalle analogue clock. The body was given *insonorizzazione generale* – sound damping by Silent Travel. The exterior of the car had new light alloy wheel rims with Michelin MXV tyres.

Production was erratic; by the end of 1982, only 1,858 Biturbos had been built. In the following year this more than doubled to 4,473. In 1984, coupé output went down to 2,497, possibly slowed by the introduction that year of the four-door 425 (*see* Chapter 5).

Maurizio Tabucchi, in his comprehensive work on the Maserati marque, points out that the early faults that dogged the first Biturbos provoked bitter criticism by the Italian motoring public. It was divided into those who accused Maserati of having betrayed their clientele with a product that failed to live up to its promises and those who admired the considerable technical and aesthetic qualities that placed the Biturbo on a higher plane than its rivals.

Nevertheless, a reputation for fragility had been established, which was to dog the Biturbo for most of its life, particularly in the USA where most exports ended up. The American *Automobile* magazine referred to it in 2005 as 'the unlovely, notoriously unreliable, and ultimately unloved Biturbo. In 1991, Maserati slinked (sic) away from the United States, and Americans hardly noticed.'

This remark has to be put into context, as both Alfa Romeo and Fiat had pulled out of America. Fiat, in particular, had a bad press, which tended to stigmatize all Italian cars. There had been a disastrous attempt to launch the Strada in North America, which led to three recalls in 1979 for suspension, fuel line and wiring problems. It was said that rather than standing for Fabbrica Italiana Automobili Torino, Fiat really meant 'Fix It Again, Tony'. Even the Germans had an acronym, *Fehler In Allen Teilen* (Faults In All Parts).*

Reliability issues were certainly to blame, but the Italians also had pressing problems at home and it was to be many years before Maserati was able to return to America.

*After Fiat's withdrawal, they were imported unofficially into America by Malcolm Bricklin, whose own ill-fated Canadian-built Bricklin sports car disappeared in the 1970s. He brought in the Fiat Spider 2000, the X-1/9 and the appalling Fiat-based Yugo, built by Zastava in Yugoslavia. The venture was not a success. Bricklin announced in December 2004 that he was going to import up to 250,000 Chinese-made cars annually beginning in 2007.

3 The Biturbo's mechanics

Pop open the bonnet of an early 1980s Biturbo and you see one of the most idiosyncratic engines in the world – the world's first twin turbo in series production, with an aluminium airbox adorned with the Maserati trident dominating the top of a V6. What can't be seen is what is inside this sealed plenum chamber: a single twin-choke, down-draught Weber carburettor. Also hardly visible are the twin IHI RHB-51 turbos, which nestle either side of the block, tucked away beneath the exhaust manifolds and pushing air under pressure though chromed ducts into the Weber.

The motor industry had come quite late to turbocharging, considering that the first experiments had begun in the early twentieth century, as it was not until 1962 that General Motors used the technique for the first time on cars – in the Chevrolet Corvair and the Oldsmobile Jetfire. It was even later that European carmakers began to adopt it – BMW in the 2002 in 1974 and then Porsche the following year.

The advantages rapidly became clear, even though a sceptical public was slow to accept turbocharging. Using exhaust gases to drive the turbos that forced more of the air/petrol mixture into the cylinders allowed higher torque at low speed, reduced emissions and boosted the power of small-capacity engines. For instance in the Lotus Esprit, a supercar that contested the Biturbo's ground, adding a single turbocharger mounted on the clutch housing boosted the power of the type 907 engine of the late 1970s from 160bhp to 210bhp.

The Biturbo's units operated at enormous speeds. There were two turbines in each turbocharger. The exhaust gases turned the first turbine at anything up to 150,000rpm, which then drove the second turbine within the casing, which compressed the air/fuel mixture in the inlet manifold.

So why did the Biturbo use two small turbochargers rather than one large one? 'Not, as sceptics may assume for one-upmanship, but because it's more efficient', declared Maserati publicity.

The original project, labelled the Maserati 2000, had a normally aspirated two-litre V6 engine, but this proved to be puny by Maserati standards.

The inception of the turbo came almost by mistake. The technical director, Giordano Casarini, an ex-Ferrari man, had joined Maserati in 1976 after some years in America, running a racing team and turbocharging Ferraris for customers. He had worked closely with George Spears, one of the founders of Spearco in the United States, who still make intercoolers and at that time offered turbo kits for the VW Golf using the Japanese IHI turbo.

Turbo experiments

Back in Modena, Casarini experimented with a German KKK supercharger mounted on the engine of a yellow three-litre Merak SS, a car that still exists in a collection in the city:

> It was more or less a toy and I was driving out of the factory gates flat out one day as De Tomaso was driving in. Later he said 'what the f– was that – I didn't give you permission to do it', but he jumped in and enjoyed it. Some Americans came

The small IMI turbochargers ran at up to 150,000rpm, but were very reliable.

The turbo inlet (arrowed) was tucked away under the exhaust manifolds.

to see him and he took them out in the car. Eventually he said, 'can we do something similar for this 2000 engine?'

In his experimental department, Casarini began two projects, the Monoturbo and the Biturbo, whose names speak for themselves. The Monoturbo had the turbo mounted at the top of the engine, but this had created excess heat: 'There were red-hot pipes all over the engine', it was reported later. The solution to reducing the run of the hot exhaust pipes to the turbo was to mount two of them low down, either side of the V6. This required them to be small but powerful, and Casarini obtained series 51 IHI turbos from George Spears for the experiments. Their success led to the new engine, titled AM452/09, being adopted as well as giving a name to the new car.

Apart from a marketing benefit in making the name Biturbo sound unusual and powerful

(owners can be thankful that an American suggestion to call it a Mini Maserati was rejected) there were other advantages in having two turbo units, which Audi were also to claim much later for their twin-turbo S4. Two small units responded more rapidly, giving higher torque at low engine speeds and the short distance between the turbos and each bank of the exhaust manifolds meant that the exhaust gases did not lose as much force as if they had to travel in long tracts from a single turbo. Experiments had shown that the load on the turbo bearings was four times less than on a single turbo, so there was less inertia to overcome and subsequently less throttle lag. In fact, Maserati claimed that all Formula One cars of the time had chosen the same solution, which reduced inertia by 75 per cent. The MABC monitored the flow to keep boost pressure below 11psi.

No doubt, had today's sophisticated engine management systems been available, Maserati would have fitted one large and one small turbo – as in the 2005 BMW 535d – in which the big one kicks in when the small has reached its limit.

At the launch, Maserati's managing director, Aurelio Bertocchi, maintained that the turbo boost would start at 2,000rpm and be 'so gentle that it is difficult to tell when it comes in'. The output statistics were impressive for a two-litre engine: 180bhp at 6,000rpm and 188lb/ft of torque at 3,500rpm. Porsche-type performance figures were claimed: 0–62 mph (0–100km/h) in 6.5sec and a maximum of 133.6mph (215km/h). Maserati looked as if they had a winner with their unusual engine.

The engine's history

When Citroën took over Maserati in 1968 to build the engine for their own grand tourer, the Paris-assembled SM, it was clear that the existing Maserati engines were not suitable for the French requirements. The six-cylinder in-line engine from the Mistral was far too big and heavy, as was their huge V8, which had sustained the product line for many years. The SM was designed to be a sleek, front-wheel-drive car, which therefore needed a low bonnet line.

The point has been made that Maserati practice was always to build the car around the engine; in the case of the SM, the engine had to fit the car. Maximum weight was decreed to be 140kg (308lb). An additional complication was that any engine had to have a capacity of below 2800cc, as the French tax system heavily penalized cars that exceeded the government's artificial 15 horsepower rating. It was not just French drivers who were hampered by archaic taxes on engine capacity: the situation in Italy was worse, with big increases starting after the 2-litre mark. Road tax went up, but more significantly the purchase tax on new cars above 2 litres soared from 18 per cent to 30 per cent.

One apocryphal version of the engine's development story says that to meet the French demands Maserati's chief engineer, Giulio Alfieri, was given six months to produce it, but he did it in three weeks by chopping two cylinders off the 4136cc engine that powered the Maserati Indy. This now made a V6 of 3102cc, but this was still too large, so the bore and stroke were reduced further to make it 2670cc, though later, for the American and some European markets, there was a 2965cc version available, mainly with an automatic gearbox.

To compromise still further, the engine had to be installed in the SM the other way around compared with the traditional layout, otherwise it would not mate with the Citroën transmission.

Another version of the engine development tale suggests that Alfieri – 'the greying whizz-kid', as he was once described in *Motor* – had designed a much smaller 3-litre V8 for a car that was never built and which had a different camshaft drive to the Indy's, and it was this version that was the basis of the V6.

Optimal angle

Whichever story is correct, the crucial fact is that the Citroën engine and the Biturbo that

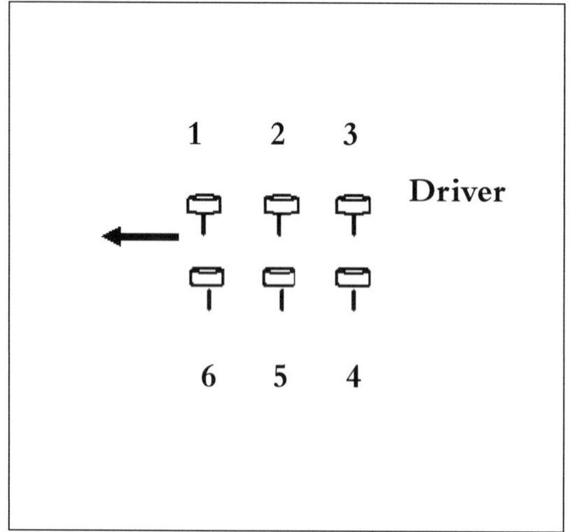

Firing order.

followed it had an included angle between the banks of cylinders of 90 degrees. But this is the optimal angle for a V8 engine, not a V6. As a V8 fires, stresses on the crankshaft from the two opposing banks of pistons are practically cancelled, vibration is reduced and the engine runs smoothly. There are four crankpins on the crankshaft, which are each shared between the two opposing pistons. A V6, however, runs smoothest with an included angle of 60 degrees; if the angle is 90 degrees there will be rough running, so there is a requirement for offset crankshaft weights to balance the firing cycle. The Biturbo's firing order was 1–6–2–5–3–4 and cylinder 1 was to the driver's right when he was seated.

The Biturbo engine had the same V6 configuration as the unit that Maserati developed for this mid-engined Merak in the early 1970s. It was a lot less accessible than the Biturbo's.

Maserati V6 engines

	Citroën SM – *tipo* C114/01	**Merak – Italian market *tipo* AM 114.62.20**	**Biturbo – 1982 *tipo* AM 452.09**
Size	2670cc	1999cc	1996cc
Bore	87mm	80mm	82mm
Stroke	75mm	66.3mm	63mm
Output	170bhp@5,500rpm	170bhp@6,000rpm	180bhp@6,000rpm

So the Citroën SM ended up with part of a V8, a successful but compromised engine, which in the Maserati designation was *tipo* C114/01, with a bore and stroke of 87 × 75mm, putting out 170bhp at 5,500rpm. This carburetted version could reach 135mph (217km/h); the C114/03 injection version was slightly faster.

This was Maserati's first V6, even though the factory got confused about this at times. It once claimed in a press release for the Ghibli that the first V6 had been built in 1958 for the 'Eldorado' raced at Monza by Stirling Moss in 1958. It was in fact a 4190cc V8, which can clearly be seen in pictures of the time.

The engine was revised for the 2+2 Maserati Merak, which had entered production in 1972 and relied on Citroën instruments and brakes. This had the V6 of 2965cc with a wider bore of 91.6mm but the same 75mm stroke. Then there was another tax-dodging 2-litre version for the Italian market, which was 1999cc, achieved with a bore of 80mm and a stroke of 66.3mm.

For the 2-litre Biturbo both bore and stroke were slightly reduced even further to 82 × 63mm, which gave a capacity of 1996cc, but

Why a V6?

The V6 engine has been favoured for many front-wheel-drive cars because it is light and short, and allows a low bonnet line. It was originally an Italian concept, first dreamt of by Lancia in the 1920s, but not put into series production until their wonderful Aurelia in 1951, which was the world's first V6-engined car. It was Lancia's Francesco De Virgilio who defined for the first time the optimal angle of 60 degrees between the cylinder banks of the 1754cc engine, which had a single chain-driven central camshaft and one Solex twin-choke carburettor.

Chrysler engineers in Detroit had experimented with all sorts of inline and V engines during and after the war, using different exhaust and intake valve combinations, and had rejected the 90-degree V6 because it lacked smoothness. No-one showed any interest in following Lancia's example until 1962, when General Motors introduced the 3800 series from 1962. It was the first V6 in an American car, a Buick 198cu in engine, derived from a 215cu in V8, and has been voted one of the best ten engines of the 20th century, despite being known as the 'odd-fire' because of its rough running.

There have been other examples of V8 projects that became 90-degree V6 engines. In Europe, the most notable was the so-called Douvrin engine, named after the French town where it was built. It was a joint engine-building venture between Peugeot, Renault and Volvo, based on a cancelled V8 project that eventually produced a V6 unit that powered, among other cars, the Renault 25 and the De Lorean.

An example of a purpose-built V6 was the highly successful Ford range of Essex and Cologne engines, which had the correct included angle of 60 degrees, as did the Alfa 75 of 1987, which had a V6 3-litre engine. Ferrari used a V6 for the Dino race car and subsequently for the Fiat Dino road version.

So why didn't Citroën build a proper new V6 with a 60-degree angle? The reason is probably the cost of tooling as the Maserati factory was already set up to machine 90-degree engines; it also suited Citroën's designs for the SM's low bonnet line, as a 90-degree engine is by nature flatter than a 60-degree one.

there is hardly any similarity in the metal with the Citroën engine. In fact, the only common part is the crankshaft rear main oil seal.

Aurelio Bertocchi was once quoted as saying that they had built more than 20,000 V6 engines for the SM and Merak; statistics seem to suggest that it was fewer than 15,000, but the point was well made that they had considerable experience of the V6 when it came to powering the Biturbo.

Despite some similarities in the bottom half of the light alloy block with its four thin-wall crankshaft bearings, there were substantial differences at the top of the engine. The chain drive of the C114 engine was replaced with a toothed rubber belt driving one camshaft in each bank of cylinders rather than two, the three Weber DCNF carburettors were replaced with the single turbo-fed Weber DCNVH 36 and the cylinder heads themselves were quite different.

Three-valve head

Instead of two valves per cylinder there were now three – two small intake and one larger exhaust. Aurelio Bertocchi was at pains to point out that this new cylinder head owned nothing to the V6 of his predecessor in charge of the factory, Giulio Alfieri.

Development had begun in the late 1970s at the De Tomaso Research Centre at Modena and took three years. The three-valve configuration could be traced back to experiments that Maserati had done on a four-cylinder engine between 1949 and 1950. There had been versions with two, three and four valves per cylinder.

According to Bertocchi, interviewed soon after the Biturbo's launch, there were definite gains in going from two to three valves, but a fourth could not be included in the new 2-litre engine because of cooling problems – though it is more likely that the complexity of the valve gear was the reason at that time. This was to change in later years, and indeed there is a tale that a 24-valve version of the V6 from the Citroën SM had already been used by the French constructor, Ligier, for their racing JS2s in the mid-1970s.

The advantage of the three-valve configuration – which the Biturbo brochure pointed out was a De Tomaso-Maserati patent – was said to be that the paired intake valves overcame the inefficiency of turbo charging at low revs, allowing a good mixture speed and swirl at low speed, but were able to deliver plenty of flow at high revs. In fact Maserati claimed that the power of this 2-litre engine could be compared to that of a 3.5 litre.

The three-valve combustion chamber – two inlet and one exhaust valve – could be traced back to Maserati experiments in the 1950s. It was designed to get the mixture in and out of the cylinder as soon as possible. It seems scarcely possible that the same space was later crammed with six valves in a development engine.

The pistons ran in liners in the light alloy block. (Mike Roberts)

There were apparently some experiments done with a system designed to save fuel, which allowed the engine to start and run on one intake valve, then switched in the second when more power was needed. This complicated electro-mechanical device was never put into production, though it is said to be the reason why the engines had inlet tracts to each valve, rather than one duct feeding both valves.

The head and block were cast by FondMetal outside Bergamo, a company best known now for its Formula One wheels, that also supplied road wheels to Maserati.

The valves bore on bucket tappets operated by a single overhead camshaft in each light alloy cylinder bank. The cylinders themselves had removable wet cylinder liners treated with a Nigusil chrome-hardening coating, developed by the German firm Mahle in the mid-1960s. It was called Nikasil by BMW and Audi, but De Tomaso had adopted it for his Moto Guzzi motorcycles and claimed it as his patent.

Manual choke

When the Biturbo began production, it was one of the few very fast cars still relying on a manual choke carburettor – and a single Weber at that, even though it was aided by the turbos. Simple, but efficient, claimed the Biturbo brochure, though one magazine described it as 'a crudity' on an engine of this type as other performance car manufacturer were enthusiastically embracing fuel injection, pioneered by Bosch for the Mercedes 300 SL as long ago as 1954.

Car and Driver went further: 'Compared with even a mediocre fuel injection system, this Quirks R Us setup is a couple of centuries behind the times.' It has to be said, though, that most of the other injected cars were not turbo-fed, which posed different problems.

It was ironic that Biturbo was still relying on the carburettors of Messrs Weber of Bologna, as Maserati had been the first Italian manufacturer to use fuel injection on road cars, following racing experience in the mid-1950s, first offering it as an option on the V8 5000GTI Series II and later as standard on the Sebring and Mistrale. But this Lucas system, which ran at 100psi, was noted for its unreliability and gave only a small increase in power. Other manufacturers such as Lancia and BMW were to use the Kugelfischer system with more success.

Because of the Lucas injection problems, many cars were converted back to three Weber 42DCOE8 carburettors, and the scarring experience of their cars' unreliable injection system was probably why Maserati virtually abandoned the principle for more than a decade; the SM engine did have Bosch injection as standard from 1972, but that was a decision by Citroën rather than Maserati's traditionalists.

Bertocchi had decided views on the reliability of fuel injection, no doubt coloured by De Tomaso's refusal to adopt it:

> When you have a problem with the fuel injection, you stop, you don't go. With the Webers, if you have a problem, each mechanic (sic) can adjust a little – but you always go.

But this would not have been the case with the Biturbo, since as the Weber was sealed in a box there was little chance of fiddling with it: the box had to be removed even to adjust the idling.

Petrol boiled

While the cast aluminium plenum chamber containing the twin-choke Weber was a thing of beauty to regard, high temperatures built up in the sealed box. 'This poor carburettor got so hot that the petrol boiled', said Giordano Casarini. This led inevitably to fuel vaporization in the carburettor, making hot starting difficult.

The plenum chamber removed to show the suffering single Weber carburettor beneath. (Mike Roberts)

Modena magic

Every Biturbo and V8 engine built at Modena was tested on one of twelve dynamometers for 2½ hours. First there was thirty minutes at idle, then an hour at 2,000rpm with turbo engaged, then another thirty minutes at 3,000rpm with a light load on the turbo, and then a final burst of two or three minutes at peak revs of between 5,500–6,000rpm.

By 1985, Maserati had a new automated machining line for blocks, cylinder heads and camshafts, which had been designed inhouse and built by a Padua company. It reduced production time significantly, as tool changes were made automatically.

The line could turn out the equivalent of eighty engines – V6 or V8 – in twenty-four hours, and could run with only one worker per shift tending it. Alongside was a second, older line that could produce forty-three engines on three shifts using three men per shift. The plant manager, Francesco Verganti, was reported in *Ward's Auto World* as saying:

> Normally you design an engine, try out a few prototypes and then you have to wait a year and a half or two years to test the engine and buy machines to make them. Using flexible machines, it now takes only one month from zero to full production. We only have to change the clamping pieces and software.

Maserati was said to be secretive about the new machining line: outsiders were carefully screened and cameras forbidden. After Ferrari gutted the factory to build the new generation 3200 coupé, they installed five dynamometer cells on which each engine was run for four hours.

Another attempt to reduce the chamber temperature was to install a pump triggered by a thermal switch to evacuate the hot gas, but it was not until the carburettor was abandoned in favour of Weber multi-point fuel injection that the solution was reached. This happened on the 1986 cars in Italy and the 1988 British models. It was not for want of trying that this was not done earlier, as Casarini said:

> De Tomaso was very stubborn, and trying to get him to change his mind was a nightmare. It was a long battle as we had said from the beginning that this car needs fuel injection and intercoolers.

There was a suspicion that, apart from De Tomaso's insistence on being right, there was a shortage of resources to carry out improvements, but they were eventually forced on him by US emission regulations.

Over the Biturbo years there was a confusing number of engine variations and mechanical changes, though the same bottom end, which is very tough, was used right up to and including the 330bhp Ghibli Cup. The changes are dealt with in the chapters relating to the various models, but essentially there were three types of the V6: the early carburettor version, the later fuel-injected version and the final four-valve cylinder head.

They came in three sizes: 2-, 2.5- and 2.8 litre, and there were further variations of intercoolers and catalysts, depending on where the cars were being sold.

Despite this confusion, Maserati have produced only five types of engines for road cars in their entire history to the present day: the in-line six from 1959, the famous four-cam V8, two V6s – one for Citroën, one for the Biturbo – and finally the V8 in today's range.

The brakes

There were servo-assisted ATE discs on all four wheels, with four-piston calipers on the front. This was because there was a dual circuit for the hydraulics, with one circuit working on all four wheels and the other on the front brakes only. The handbrake worked separately in drums at the rear, in an attempt to avoid the problems that Jaguars and other cars had with rear discs where the handbrake effort was on two tiny pads on the discs, often giving insufficient friction to hold a heavy car on a slope. It did not seem to work in all cases. One test of the 425 saloon described the handbrake as 'an unmitigated disaster incapable of resisting the slightest gradient', though this may have been more of a maintenance problem than a design fault.

Later there would be noises made about the lack of an anti-lock braking system, but at the time of the launch it was a relatively new device, having been pioneered by Bosch on the 1978 Mercedes-Benz 450SEL 6.9. However, it did take ten years to appear on the Biturbo, as it was not until 1993 that it was fitted.

Suspension and steering

The suspension was independent all round by coil spring struts and relied on the works of Earl MacPherson at the front and Colin Chapman at the rear. The MacPherson strut, which is now almost universal, was a departure for Maserati from their usual practice of upper and lower arms. The Chapman set-up at the rear was designed originally for the Lotus Elite – and it consisted of semi-training wishbones attached to the sprung strut. Because of its effectiveness and the car's low centre of gravity, Maserati claimed that there was no need for a rear anti-roll bar, though there was one at the front.

There was mounting criticism of the fact that anti-lock brakes were not fitted to such a powerful car. It took ten years for the Bosch unit (seen here at the right of the engine bay) to be fitted.

The thirty-six-valve engine

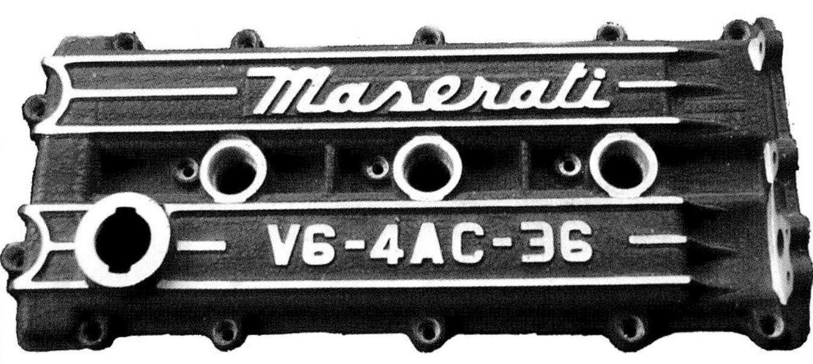

The cam cover tells the story: four overhead camshafts, thirty-six valves, all in a 2.0-litre engine. Would it have ever worked?

In the summer of 1985, Maserati announced that they were working on a two-seater sports car. It would be light – 1,870lb (850kg), which was more than 440lb (200kg) less than the Biturbo coupé – and have a 250bhp engine.

'Exciting news', declared the publicity in *Maserati Hi-Tech* some months later. The car would be powered by a new twin-turbo, dohc, six-valves-per-cylinder V6. This was a formidable achievement, bearing in mind that Aurelio Bertocchi had declared a few years earlier that the Biturbo engine had only three valves per cylinder because it was not possible to put in four. And all thirty-six valves were to be in a 1996cc displacement engine, ready to go into this new *sei valvole* sports car, which would be officially announced in 1986. Maximum power was now said to be 261bhp at 7,200rpm, which made it very high revving compared with the normal V6 maximum of 6,250rpm.

The factory said it would offer 'the sheer pleasure of driving a car that combines the prestige of a glorious sporting tradition with avant-garde technology'. Cynics might have remarked that they would prefer Maserati to get the existing technology right first.

A six-valves-per-cylinder, quad-cam head was almost unheard of because of the complexity of casting and timing – four valves did what most manufacturers of the time needed – but Maserati went ahead anyway on the basis that the faster the fuel charge mixture could be pumped into the cylinders, the more performance could be attained.

The engine was designated the 6.36, for obvious reasons. There were three inlet and three exhaust valves, which sounds obvious, but multi-valve engines can have strange configurations: the Audi RS6 and RS8, for instance, have five valves, three inlets and two exhausts. (It is said that Audi considered six valves but discovered that they offered less valve seat length than the five-valve.)

With six valve seats ringing each combustion chamber, there was no room for anything else except the central spark plug. These chambers were claimed to operate at low temperatures because of the efficient coolant flow in the head, but the heat generated must have been enormous. The central valves of the three inlets and of the three exhausts were inclined at different angles to give swirl in the combustion chamber. There was said to be a higher compression ratio than in the standard engine, though this was not specified.

There was an ingenious and simple method of valve operation, which Maserati patented: the overhead cam bore on a flat plate that linked all three valves in the cylinder head together, spreading the load and pushing them down simultaneously. Maserati called this 'finger control', claiming that its designers had avoided all possible complications and intricate parts, which would inevitably make an engine more delicate and 'unacceptable on today's automobile market'. The rest was standard Biturbo, having watercooled turbos, with the boost restricted to 0.8 bar.

Alas, neither the engine nor the car was ever produced. 'It was all bullshit', says Giordano Casarini. 'People were talking of five-valve engines and De Tomaso said he wanted six – to have more than the others'.

Nevertheless, the quad-cam experiment would stand Maserati in good stead for the four-valve engine, which was to appear for the first time at the Turin motor show in 1998. This was to put out 245bhp – not far off the *sei valvole*'s 261bhp – without the complications of the six-valve configuration.

At the same time as the *sei valvole* was announced there were also hints of yet another new car, a V8 mid-engined prototype, which could be ready in 1988. This, too, failed to appear.

The six-valve engine is still on display at the refurbished Maserati factory.

Steering was conventional rack and pinion, 4.1 turns lock-to-lock, manual at first then from 1985 offered with power steering.

Transmission

The five-speed manual gearbox was from Zahnradfabrik Friedrichshafen in Germany and had the familiar racing dog-leg pattern beloved of Italian high-speed drivers. First gear was opposite reverse, enabling rapid straight changes in the higher gears, particularly from fifth to fourth – fine for fast driving, but a dogleg into first can be a real pain in heavy traffic. It was fairly low-geared with fifth gear (0.87:1) producing 20.2mph per 1,000rpm.

The initial automatic offering was the ZF 3HP 22 box with three forward speeds. From 1985 there was a three-speed Borg-Warner auto available, which was upgraded to a four-speed ZF auto with the introduction of the 2.8-litre models. Later, Getrag five-speed manual gearboxes appeared.

Power was transmitted to a Salisbury axle, which the makers, GKN, had originally specified for a Morgan. It contained a 12 HU differential with a ratio of 3.73:1 and was mounted on the same rubber-insulated subframe that supported the rear struts. With automatic transmission the final drive ratio became 3.31:1. The Salisbury axle internals were later replaced by a Sensitork limited slip differential, and later still by the Maserati Ranger differential.

Wheels and tyres

Rather fussy light alloy 14in rims carried Pirelli Cinturatos of 195/60 front and rear. For winter use, Pirelli 190s of 185/65 were recommended.

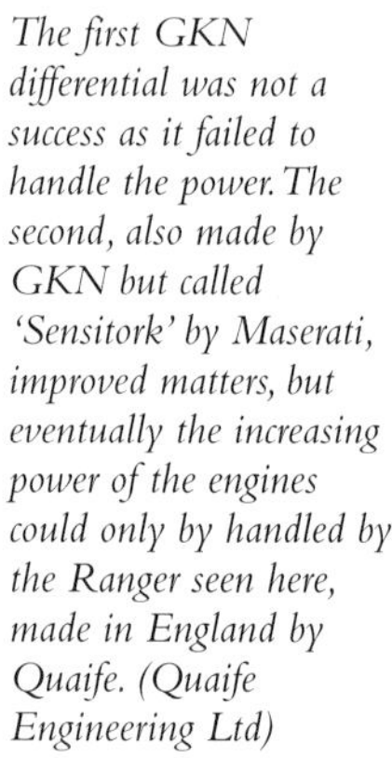

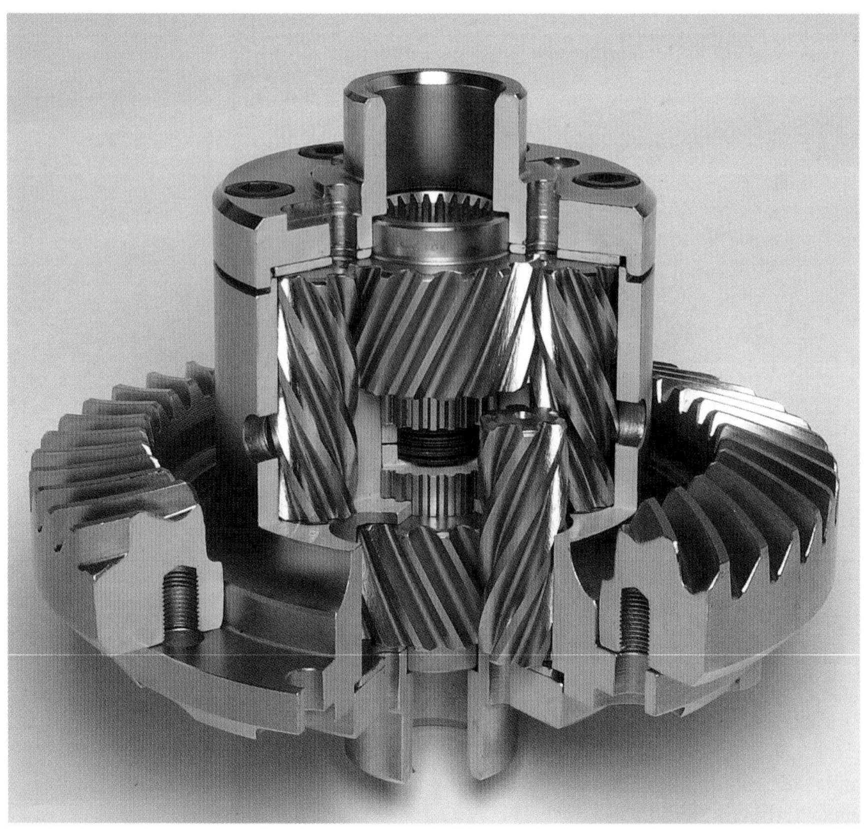

The first GKN differential was not a success as it failed to handle the power. The second, also made by GKN but called 'Sensitork' by Maserati, improved matters, but eventually the increasing power of the engines could only by handled by the Ranger seen here, made in England by Quaife. (Quaife Engineering Ltd)

4 The 2.5 and intercooling

As with many tycoons, modesty was an unknown virtue to Alejandro De Tomaso. He was determined that everyone should know of his part in creating the Biturbo, even to the extent of putting this signed personal message in the drivers' manuals:

> Dear Sir (sic)
>
> When I designed the 'Biturbo', I put in this fascinating task all my personal experience as racing driver and manufacturer of sports and racing cars, thus making the dream come true of everybody who – like me – wants to drive a car which combines all the modern comforts with a great (sic) roadholding, a chassis highly reliable under any circumstance, brakes which never fade even after extensive use and an extraordinary Maserati power unit.
>
> I am sure that all the care, the enthusiasm and the sacrifices we have poured into this car will be rewarded by the pleasure and satisfaction this 'Biturbo' will bring you.
>
> A new 'era' of car enthusiasts has now started.
>
> A De Tomaso
> OFFICINE A MASERATI S.p.A.

The last line of the text is a clumsy rendition of what appeared in the Italian handbooks: *Apre ora un dialogo tra appassionati di automobili* – 'a passionate automobile dialogue' sounds a lot better than 'a new era'. As the model range grew, De Tomaso replaced 'Biturbo' in the text with whatever version was next, thus claiming personally to have designed most of the range.

The Biturbo E

The first of many variations on the Biturbo theme came in the autumn of 1983, when an uprated engine of 2.5 litres was announced for export markets only, principally for the United States. With an obvious eye on the American predilection for large engines, De Tomaso claimed that his new engine's power and torque were the equivalent of a 4-litre normally aspirated engine.

When the Biturbo E arrived there in the first months of 1984, it was – just like Maseratis before it – specially modified to meet the legislation introduced in America in the 1970s to reduce emissions by strangling engine power. Makers of high-performance cars were further penalized by the 1978 'gas-guzzling' tax that was imposed on the list price of a car if it failed to meet a certain level of fuel consumption. This tax policy contrasted with Europe, where extra taxes tended to be based on engine capacity rather than consumption.

The emission laws were ever-tightening and meant that the Biturbo had to be fitted with a three-way catalyst and an air pump to meet the American restrictions. So a new 2.5-litre engine was installed to make up for the power that these sapped. Swiss market cars were also fitted with catalysers, but they did not appear on right-hand-drive UK cars until nearly ten years later when European legislation caught up with the Americans.

Bodily, the Biturbo E for the USA was much the same as the Italian version. At this stage there was no power steering or automatic gearbox offered in America, which was surprising.

(When the auto was eventually offered, it was a lacklustre three-speed, unfitted to the car's performance.) Road testing by *Car and Driver* produced a 0–60mph speed of 6.8sec, a 0–100mph of 21.4sec and a top speed of 125mph (201km/h) – figures roughly comparable to the smaller-engined European model.

The 2.5 engine

The engine was 2491cc (152cu in) and the extra capacity was achieved by widening the bore from 82mm to 91.6mm. The cylinder liners were cast iron rather than aluminium. The compression ratio was slightly lower and the unit produced 185bhp at 5,500rpm and 208lb/ft of torque at 3,000rpm, compared with the smaller engine's 180bhp at 6,000rpm and 188lb/ft at 3,500rpm. For other export markets there was also a slightly tuned version that gave 11bhp more, producing 196bhp at 5,600rpm.

The US EPA combined petrol consumption was 18mpg and the city only 15mpg. This landed every early Biturbo sent to the USA with a gas-guzzling tax bill of $450, which had to be built into the price. (This legislation persists: the Corporate Average Fuel Economy

Biturbo 2.5-litre coupé/ES/Si (1983–90)

Engine – coupé	
Type	AM453
Layout	V6 90 degrees – 3 valves per cylinder, single overhead cam per bank, two IHI turbochargers (Type AM472 as above with injection in Si from 1987)
Bore × stroke:	91.6 × 63mm
Capacity:	2491cc
Compression ratio:	7.8:1
Max power:	189bhp/141kW@5,500rpm 196bhp/146kW@5,600rpm – ES 200bhp/147kW@5,500rpm – Si
Max torque:	222.7lb ft/30.8kg m @4,400rpm
Fuel system:	Weber twin-choke carburettor; Si injection 1987
Intercoolers:	None
Transmission	
Gearbox:	ZF manual 5 speed + reverse. Automatic 3-speed option
Final drive:	Sensitork 3.73:1
Suspension	
Front:	MacPherson strut with anti-roll bar, coil springs, shock absorbers
Rear:	Trailing arms, coil springs, shock absorbers, anti-roll bar
Steering:	Power-assisted rack and pinion
Brakes:	Servo-assisted twin circuit, front and rear ventilated discs with floating calipers, rear drum parking brake.
Running gear	
Wheels:	6J × 14
Tyres:	195/60VR 14 or 205/60
Performance	
Max speed:	133mph (225km/h)
Acceleration:	0–62mph (100km/h) in 6.5sec
Dimensions	
Wheelbase:	99in (2,514mm)
Front track:	55.9in (1,420mm)
Rear track:	56.3in (1,431mm)
Length:	163.5in (4,153mm)
Width:	67.5in (1,714mm)
Height:	51.4in (1,305mm)
Weight:	2,414lb (1,095kg)
Number built:	6,100

Trident injection

The Trident injection system was a British attempt to get around the hot-starting problem.

The Biturbo's hot starting problems could have been avoided if there had been a much swifter move to fuel injection, rather than relying on the overheated Weber carburettor.

There was, in the UK in the late 1980s, an attempt to market a system known as Trident injection, specifically for the early 2½-litre cars, the aim being to avoid the hot starting problems rather than to aid performance.

Whereas the Lucas system on some of the pre-Biturbo cars had been indirect injection, this was electronic, relying on a Zytec ECU and other proprietary parts buried under a metal casting bearing the name Trident Motor Sport, the name of a company run by Nick May, who at that time also happened to be the managing director of Maserati UK.

The project was solely financed by May and the development done by Mangoletsi in Cheshire, who have been producing tuning kits since the 1960s. The original idea was to sell it as an aftermarket system costing £3,000 and, although it worked very well, its time had passed.

In late 1989 Anthony Cazalet made a trip around Europe to show it to Maserati importers. It was not a success. 'By that time the early cars to which Trident would be fitted were worth not much more than the fuel injection system was going to cost, so the cost was disproportionate and the new cars had injection anyway.'

Eventually, a dealer in Milan bought one to fit to a 2.0-litre coupé and ten others were fitted to the last of the carburetted cars that Maserati UK had in stock.

rules for 2005 required that each car manufacturer met a federal standard of 27.5mpg across the range of cars they make. These rules discriminate against makers with a small range of high-performance cars like Maserati; in 2005, breaches of the rules cost Ferrari Maserati North America Inc. $1.5m and BMW more than $12m.)

So with the tax, the Biturbo was a $25,000 (£17,850) car, when a Detroit-built Ford Thunderbird turbo could be had for about half the price, and a Mercedes-Benz 190E 2.3 for around $22,000 (£15,700).

In 1981, the year before the Biturbo, 555 cars had been made by Maserati; the next year production at 2,265 (1,858 of them Biturbos) was even higher than Ferrari, and in 1984 it rose to 6,180. These figures include, of course, some of the Merak, Kyalami and Quattroporte models, which were still being catalogued by *Quattroruote* in 1984.

Profits went upwards as production rose. In the first ten months of 1983 they were around £1 million. The following year they soared to £7.5 million. The launch of the Biturbo finally achieved what De Tomaso had planned for the company back in 1975. Maserati started making a profit and production was greatly increased.

By January 1984, production was running at forty Biturbos a day and by October, 3,400 cars had been exported – the majority of that year's production. In the three years following the launch, 9,000 cars were made in total. Prices soon began to rise, but did not deter American buyers: 2,000 Biturbos were sold there in 1984 and 2,200 the following year, well above 50 per cent of the Lambrate factory's output.

There was, however, a problem with these US cars, which was to come to light in 1987 after a customer reported smouldering and smoking. It was due to the exhaust emissions equipment fitted to the US cars, the habit of leaving cars to warm up unattended and possibly the unfamiliarity of their drivers with the hand-operated choke. The car's operations manual specifically stated that the choke should be pushed home as soon as possible after starting a cold engine – and not to let the car run at a fast idle for two or three minutes as this could damage the exhaust emission system. On the 1984 and 1985 cars there was even an orange dashboard light marked CHOKE, to warn when it was operating. In April 1988, Randal K. Busick, vice president of Maserati Automobiles Inc., reported to the National Highways and Transportation Authority in Washington that recall of these cars was necessary.

'The possibility of fire'

> There have been occurrences ... where the exhaust system has become so overheated that the vehicles' undercoating has begun to smolder [sic] and smoke. There have been reported cases where passenger compartment interior materials have also been scorched. This condition presents the possibility of fire. There have been no injuries reported.

A letter was sent to owners of the 1984/5 cars outlining the problem and asking for them to return their cars to dealers for a modification kit for the exhaust system, which would take an hour and a half to install. With this in place the engine could be run with the choke out without causing damage. It seems the nub of the problem was that the catalyst overheated and the rubber rings holding the exhaust to the body caught fire and dropped off.

The recall to owners affected 3,724 cars. By July 1989, 3,594 had been repaired, 113 cars had been sold on to other owners, for whom presumably there was no address, and 128 notices were returned as being undeliverable.

This was probably the final straw for Maserati, leading to the decision to withdraw from the American market in 1991. Apart from reliability issues there was a fear of expensive litigation, no doubt prompted by the recall of cars likely to combust. Dott. Eugenio Alzati, who ran Maserati in the early 1990s, was quoted as saying:

> We will go back to the US when there's legislation to protect the manufacturer as well as the customer – you can't spend the company's entire budget in court being sued by a single client.

When Ferrari took over Maserati in 1997, one of their executives admitted that they had pulled out because of all the quality and reliability problems that the Biturbo had in the De Tomaso days. He went on:

> I think it was a good decision because the North American market is a very demanding market that demands quality and enormous reliability, 100 per cent reliability, things that Maserati was not able to offer ten years ago.
>
> Ten years have passed and we are back into the business. We have a very good product; we have committed ourselves to a maximum goal of 100 per cent reliability, 100 per cent quality, etc., that was really the main objective of the new Ferrari management here at Maserati.

Right-hand-drive delays

While exports to America and the rest of Europe went steaming ahead, the right-hand-drive countries like Britain, Australia, South Africa, Hong Kong, Malaysia, Singapore and Thailand were bereft of Biturbos. From the January 1981 launch *Autocar* had reported: 'Right-hand drive versions of the Biturbo will not be available for a year or so.'

By April 1983 the same magazine disclosed that no right-hand-drive cars had yet been built. 'As so often happens with this Italian specialist', it sighed, 'the prototypes were shown a long time before they were ready for production.' *Car* magazine had been equally bullish in March 1982:

> When the 2.0-litre Biturbo makes its debut in right-hand drive in the middle of next year, the total of Maserati cars (sold in Britain) will leap from twenty-five cars a year to about 500. Instead of the cars being sold by half-a-dozen garages, there will be upwards of thirty dealerships.

This mystic figure of thirty dealers was to appear and disappear over the years without ever being achieved, let alone sales of several hundred.

The delay in right-hand-drive production had serious effects for the British importer, Modena Concessionaires, part of International Motors of West Bromwich, because the Merak, Khamsin and Kyalami were all stopping production. Eventually they had no Maseratis left to sell, and gave up the franchise. In fact the Biturbo 1, as it became known, was never sold through dealers in the UK. In 1984 there were only three in Britain – two 2.0-litres and one 2.5, all imported privately. Said *Motor*, which got its hands on a German-registered 2.5:

> Alas, Alessandro (sic) De Tomaso's Maserati for the masses is unlikely ever to go on sale in the UK. It seems he is totally uninterested in building rhd models, despite pleas from UK distributors.

In Germany the car was now selling at the equivalent of £13,000 – more than a BMW 525i would cost in Britain.

Motor's test produced some very mixed results and would not have been encouraging for those who were still waiting patiently for a right-hand-drive version, as its verdict was that the Biturbo was a fine car with a catalogue of problems, though it had undeniable appeal, with terrific performance dressed in Italian clothes. It concluded: 'In Italy the model is reckoned to be a success and pretty reliable. It was great – while it lasted.'

So what led to this dismissive verdict? The test had come to an abrupt end when a loosening distributor caused faulty ignition timing that led to a holed piston. This was said to be a known fault. And the back window was about to pop out. This was originally bonded into place and covered with a rubber seal as a finisher.

Before that the testers had been unhappy with the suspension; they reckoned that the semi-trailing arms at the rear were at too acute an angle, which led to lurching when lifting off on a bend. (Owners found that this unpredictable handling was to lead to many spins and spills, and it was not unknown in America for sandbags to be put in the boot to keep the rear end more stable.)

Missoni interior

The engine and its wonderful exhaust note were praised as was the thoroughly modern interior, which used only the minimum of plastics. There was not, however, the lavish interior by the Italian fashion designers Missoni, which was fitted in the 2.0-litre Italian Biturbo: other European versions had corduroy-type upholstery. And the sharp-eyed testers detected that the control stalks, gauges and grab handles were sourced from the Lancia Delta.

Given all these reservations, perhaps it was just as well that it was another two and half years before the first officially imported cars, the Biturbo IIs, arrived in Britain. The original model was never sold in the UK, though some were imported and there may have been a tiny number made to special order. The stated reason for the delay was that Maserati wanted to consolidate European and American markets before building a right-hand-drive car, though some scepticism was expressed at De Tomaso's strategy by British buyers anxious to get their hands on the car; they thought he could probably sell all he could make without having to re-tool for a right-hand-drive model. One of the many British importers of Maseratis estimated that right-hand drive added £1,500 to the factory gate price.

Apart from *Motor*, British motor magazines had scarcely bothered over the years to mention a car that could not be bought in the UK, so impressions in English of the first years of the Biturbo come mainly from America, where it was thoroughly tested by publications such as *Road & Track*, which in June 1984 put it up against a BMW 325e that had the in-line six of 2693cc. There were superficial similarities: they were both upmarket, compact sporting saloons with six-cylinder engines, five-speed manual gearboxes, four-wheel disc brakes and even the same Pirelli P6 tyres.

The Biturbo came fully-equipped with air conditioning, cord or leather interior, stereo, electric windows, mirrors and sunroof as standard. The BMW had much the same, though leather cost an extra $800, but even if that were included it came in at $21,760, some $4,500 dollars cheaper than the Maserati.

Those who paid the extra got the performance. The Biturbo screamed ahead of the BMW – 0–60mph in 7.2sec compared with the BMW's 8.9sec, and 0–100mph in 22.3sec while the laggardly German took 35sec.

Road & Track's verdict was that they would choose the Maserati. The BMW was for someone more concerned with reliability, fuel economy and service availability. The Biturbo, on the other hand, was for an enthusiast who loved cars, hungered for something exotic and had a strong streak of automotive romance.

Car and Driver hated the brakes, which locked up, but thought that the cost was a small price to pay for a blue-blooded Maserati aristocrat, with 'an old-world opulent interior' and the performance to blow off almost any other modern car.

It was undoubtedly the first reviews in influential American motoring journals in the spring of 1984 that led to a surge in demand for the Biturbo in the USA. People were queuing up to buy it. In that year, 2,000 were sold, and 2,200 the following year. But it was not to last. In 1986, there were fewer than 1,200 sold and even less the following year.

The Biturbo had acquired an unfortunate reputation for being temperamental and buyers of the exotic shied away, even as Maserati were extending the Biturbo repertoire with new models. There was also the issue of parts prices – they were fantastically expensive. In September 1987, a new 2.5 engine was $10,000, a piston nearly $400 and a rear bumper $870.

Right-hand drive at last

'We have decided to come back to the UK market because it has been an important one for us for thirty years', announced Francesco Verganti of Maserati in 1986. 'Until now demand has been so strong in Italy and the US that we haven't had the capacity.' In fact, 80 per cent of production went to these two countries in 1986 and demand had been largely satisfied, so it was time to look for more markets.

Officially imported Biturbos appeared for the first time at the Birmingham Motor Show in November 1986. The Maserati UK staff were ecstatic because their stand was next to Jaguar, who were launching the new XJ6 and they hoped for spill-over from the crowds mobbing the Jaguar stand.

The draw on the Maserati stand, apart from the Biturbos, was the 1956 250F single-seater driven by Fangio. There was a gold 425, whose colour was called Old Modena, a red Spyder and a Rifle Grey coupé. Grey was De Tomaso's favourite colour and the two other right-hand-drive cars in that colour, a 425 and coupé, had earlier arrived in Britain for homologation – that is, the official recognition of a car as a production model by meeting local standards. Technical director Anthony Cazalet recalled:

> We had to do several tests and one of them was a windscreen defrost/demist at –20°C. MIRA did not have a room cold enough so we did it at British Aerospace at Stevenage.
>
> We used a 425 – it was a wonder it started in those conditions – and after about twenty minutes the car was revving flat out and smoke started pouring from the engine. I grabbed an extinguisher and put the fire out – the power steering pump had blown oil over the red-hot turbos. There was a tremendous to-do, but the windscreen had cleared – so we passed the test.

Both cars were used for further testing, some of it involving crashes; amazingly they were later repaired and sold.

The first cars to be sold to the public – three transporter loads, some fifteen to twenty – arrived in Dover in January 1987; they were to have gone to Sheerness, but the weather was too bad. Further imports began trickling in through Sheerness where a mechanic did the pre-delivery inspection – in most cases having to adjust the float level in the carburettor and check for seepage between the head and the cam carrier, which leaked oil onto the exhaust.

The importers were again forecasting a hopelessly optimistic sales figure, this time 600 a year. *Fast Lane* had been told in the autumn of 1985 that right-hand-drive coupés were planned for the UK and that the price would be in the region of £17,500. In 1986, the first right-hand-drive models were made – but only twenty-three of them. The cost in the UK, it was announced, would be £20,000 for the coupé, £23,000 for the 425 and £24,000 for the Spyder.

But when *Car* magazine got its hands on one of the first Biturbo II coupés in the autumn of 1986, the price was £23,500. This was very high – putting it in almost at the top range of sports car prices. 'This could be an Italian car that lasts', it declared hopefully, after noting this and failing to discover a single welded seam in the bodywork.

It had a smooth and potent engine, and a grippy and supple chassis (not some other testers' experience). On the other hand, it had vague steering, a wayward gear change and soft brakes. The basic trim was leatherette; the hide on the test car was an extra £700, but seemingly worth it. 'Soft leather the colour of autumn leaves swathes the seats, the doors, the dash; beige suede spans the ceiling. It's as rich as a Belgian chocolate without being as sickly.'

Fast Lane also tested the 2.5 coupé in the following spring and was mightily impressed: 'A highly covetable car … De Tomaso has exploited what the company is best at – building beautiful engines; the motor is the star of the Biturbo.' Though the power delivery was exhilarating, the engine coughed when coming off and on the throttle. However, when the turbos kicked in over 3,000rpm there was 'slingshot acceleration'.

They liked the car so much that they ran another test six months later when they again praised the silky smooth power after 3,000rpm, but criticized the bouncy ride, tricky handling in the wet and 'horrendous' petrol consumption of 16.07mpg.

The price had gone up yet again. The coupé was now £24,795, the 425 £3,000 more and the Spyder an extra £4,000. To put these figure into context, here are some other prices of the time, rounded for comparison:

Ford Escort	£5,000
Ford Sierra Cosworth	£17,500
Jaguar XJS 3.6	£19,000
BMW 535 M3	£23,500

However, *Car* magazine thought the coupé by no means costly for what it was – carefully made and beautifully finished, it was a gentleman's car, a refreshingly different grand tourer but with a frightening thirst.

Intercooling

A further high-performance Biturbo E model was offered in the USA in 1985 only; 200 were imported, each with a special numbered plaque on the dash. The car had two-tone paint – silver or red for the upper half and grey for the lower – stiffer suspension, a thicker anti-roll bar, wider wheels and tyres that were 20VR55 rather than 195VR60.

But the main change was in the engine, where optional intercoolers were offered for the first time, which boosted performance from 185bhp to 205bhp at 5,500rpm and torque went up from 208lb ft at 3,000rpm to 260lb ft. A little badge on the back declared that the car was 'Liquid intercooled'.

There were two types of intercooler available – air-to-air or air-to-liquid – both made by Spearco in conjunction with Maserati. The air-to-liquid was only for west coast of America. Essentially, both types relied on special radiators to cool the hot air from the turbochargers before it got into the engine.

The principle of intercooling is that the cooler air is denser and delivers a greater fuel/air mixture to the engine, since denser air can carry a higher charge of fuel, allowing better performance and preventing pre-ignition and detonation of the mixture, which can damage the engine.

Today's cars, such as the Subaru Impreza WRX, which has air-to-air cooling, have a bonnet scoop to force air over the intercooler radiator, while others using liquid intercooling have a water supply to a radiator that is separate from the normal cooling system.

The Spearco air-to-air system could be retrofitted to the Biturbo in about four hours. The radiator was lowered by an inch to allow for a duct to take the air into the intercooler in front of the carburettor plenum chamber. The cost was just under $900. Later versions of air-to-air intercooling relied on the ram effect created by NACA ducts in the bonnet, rather than a duct above the radiator.

The Biturbo with air-to-liquid intercooling had two tiny radiators – one for each turbo – plumbed into the inlet tract and they operated when boost pressure was above 2psi. The mixture of water and antifreeze was then pumped to a small radiator ahead of the main radiator at the front of the car.

The result of the reworking was a slight increase in performance, judging by test figures: 0–60mph in 6.73sec compared with the standard Biturbo's 7.2sec and in the standard quarter mile reaching 91.2mph (146.7km/h) rather than 88mph (142km/h).

Intercoolers also became a dealer-fitted option in Britain, with an air-to-air kit developed by Maserati UK, which was mounted on top of the cam covers. It was not satisfactory due to narrow piping and the heat generated by the engine. Intercoolers in later cars went in front of the main radiator, two small radiators, one each side.

Nevertheless, an example of how intercooling worked on the Biturbo was recorded by

Intercooling as standard was first introduced on the Biturbo S – evidenced by the ducts on the bonnet. (Fonte Archivio Maserati)

Car magazine in Britain during a test of a 2.5 in 1987. It found that on a day when the outside temperature was 3°C, the temperature at the impeller outlets was 95°C, but after passing through the intercooler matrices, the temperature dropped to less than 45°C.

Maserati maintained at the time that the intercoolers would increase reliability and engine life, and that there would be no discernible increase in performance. However, when Maserati supplied *Autocar* with a Biturbo for test through Bill McGrath, he took off the intercoolers to get a decent 0–60mph figure. They turned out to be so efficient that in winter they caused carburettor icing, making the Biturbo flat spot even worse.

Which cars had what intercoolers at any one time is, like the rest of Maserati lore, not entirely clear in all cases. But basically, other than the early Italian market Biturbo S and export ES mentioned below, the first Biturbos, 425s and Spyders had none; the Biturbo E in the USA could have dual air-to-water or air-to-air.

From the start of the injected cars, the Si, 425i and Spyder i, had air-to-air as did the 228, 430 and following cars. All 2.8 cars had intercooling as standard, and from the 222E onwards the front of the engine bay was redesigned to give better space for the units.

As to turbos, the first cars were not cooled; there was a brief flirtation with oil cooling before standardization on water-cooled units.

The Italian S

As production accelerated so did the flow of new models, which can be bewildering to follow, as there were variations in specification for the home and export markets.

After the Biturbo E, the next significant model was the 2.0-litre S, launched in Rome in

July 1983 for the domestic market in a limited series of 350. Intercoolers and an increase in turbo boost gave it an extra 25bhp, giving 205bhp at 6,500rpm. It was a slightly faster and meaner-looking version of the standard 2.0-litre Italian market coupé with stiffer suspension. The extra punch of the engine was particularly noticeable over 3,500rpm, according to *Car*: 'The little V6 races on to the 7,000rpm mark with tremendous smoothness and alacrity.'

The front grille was black with a chrome bar carrying the trident and the car came in two-tone colours, though the bottom half below the central crease was always black – matched by the black wheels with a chrome surround. The more sporting look was contributed to by wider Pirelli P7 tyres and a front spoiler with foglamps. At the rear there was a curious spoiler, which covered the whole of the boot and sloped upwards towards the rear. It was made of plastic on early cars and of rubber on later models. Interiors were tan leather or Alcantara.

There were two NACA air ducts* – first mounted low at the front, and then on the bonnet – used for air-to-air intercooling, and there was a higher top gear.

Another version of this car was made for the export market and called the Biturbo ES. It was a two-tone special with either red or silver above black.

Suede it's not

Alcantara is a *faux* suede, much used in Italian cars over the past few decades, and has often fooled magazine road testers into describing it as real leather. Its appearance and feel is not to everyone's taste, particularly combined with some of the lurid colours of the 1970s and 1980s.

The material is also used in clothing and for interior décor. It was dreamed up in the research laboratories of a Japanese company, Toray Industries, in the early 1970s as a substitute for leather. Toray went into partnership with an Italian company in Umbria in 1972 and the Alcantara factory is still in business in Italy, though now wholly Japanese-owned.

The name appears to come from the Arabic *al kantar* – the bridge – and the company maintains that it bridges two worlds: Japanese technological development and Italian skill.

Fuel injection

Production ran from 1984 to 1986 when the Biturbo i was introduced, a major step forward since it did away with the single Weber carburettor on which the cars had relied from the start, and substituted much-needed injection. This was quickly followed by the Si, which went into production in April 1987 and lasted until the introduction of the 222 in 1988. The Biturbo i had a Weber speed density fuel injection system and Magneti Marelli electronic ignition. There were versions for both Italian (2.0-litre) and export markets (2.5-litre), both equipped with intercoolers.

Fuel injection had to come, despite Bertocchi's reservations, to enable the cars to meet emission regulations in America, where it was introduced in the spring of 1987. Maserati described it as a joint project between Weber and Marelli to produce one of the most sophisticated fuel injection systems ever to be fitted to turbocharged engines. The ignition and injection systems both had separate control units, which nevertheless were linked and had a shared memory of 100,000 parameters.

The factory was so proud of this new device, which gave 'perfect engine operation and excellent performance under all conditions', that they printed possibly the most boring page ever seen in car brochures – pictures of the printed circuit boards with their transistors.

The linked system was so complex that it required two special units to service it, so dealers had to cough up several thousand pounds for the equipment. Ford also used the system in

*NACA ducts are used for engine breathing and cooling, and to push fresh air into the passenger compartment. They are named after the US National Advisory Committee for Aerodynamics, which devised low-drag air ducts for jet engines.

ABOVE: The Si range saw the consolidation of fuel injection, and a boot spoiler. The export version, the SE, had the 2.8 engine. (Fonte Archivio Maserati)

The FondMetal wheels on the SE looked fussy.

conjunction with a Garret T3 turbocharger on the Sierra Cosworth, introduced in July 1986.

There are two main types of injection: mass flow, which measures the mass of air entering the engine, and the speed density system chosen for the Biturbo, which uses the speed of the engine and the density of the air to measure engine airflow. A manifold sensor maps the speed and density against a factory-set table of efficiency. The air/fuel ratio is then checked by an oxygen sensor, which corrects any mistakes and alters the flow of fuel to the injectors.

Combined with other small changes, such as different material for the head gaskets and valve seats, injection in the Si not only made the car more tractable in traffic, but led to a large boost in power to more than 220bhp; the new Sensitork 3.31:1 limited slip differential was much better at handling the power than the original unit. The intercoolers were moved in front of the radiator, but the NACA ducts remained for effect.

Changes to the body to make the car look more aggressive included spoilers and sideskirts. From July 1987, a cruise control was available as a dealer fitment in the United States.

The Si came in three colours: blue-grey, red and black. There were new seats and interiors of leather and Alcantara, with Sienna for the red and grey cars and ivory for the black cars – which for some reason cost more.

After the initial sales surge, Biturbos became rather difficult to sell and many importers customized the car to make it look more attractive and exciting.

The British SE

In Britain, for instance, to try to shift the carburetted cars, there was the SE – which had

Biturbo for Britain. The spoilers, sideskirts and other tweaks were added in the UK to try to shift a backlog of cars. (Fonte Archivio Maserati)

The SE version of the Spyder.

In addition to sideskirts, the British SE had rubber inserts in the bumpers front and rear.

modifications across all the extant 2.5 range, the coupé, Spyder and 425. This model is not to be confused with the later 222SE.

The British market SEs had Zender side skirts (later replaced with a factory version) and front and rear spoilers, which incorporated the three pieces of black plastic from the standard bumper. 'The word spoiler was absolutely correct', according to one Maserati insider. There were fancy Momo or FondMetal wheels. The early carburettor cars had brown plastic door trims; the injection SEs had grey plastic trims.

A brochure announcing the arrival of this 2.5 SE series announced that the cars had been designed 'not by a cold-hearted scientist, but by Zagato, a design studio with a keen eye for a driver's sense of aesthetics'.

This apportioning of responsibility for the coupé and 425 styling to Zagato, who had only been credited officially with the Spyder's design, was either completely wrong, or a suggestion that they had a hand in the SE's gussied-up bits. 'The subtle, delicately pitched purr of the twin turbochargers turns heads wherever you go', said the brochure.

The injection cars arrived in Britain in 1988. 'One of the few cars that made a two-hour drive seem like ten minutes', said a Maserati advert in *Autocar* in April 1988. It claimed a 0–60mph time of 6.6sec and a top speed of more than 135mph (217km/h). Business began to be brisk, but the collapse of Maserati UK at the end of 1990 dealt a severe blow to sales.

5 The first four-door cars – the 425 and 420

One of the first things that De Tomaso had done after taking over in 1975 was to abandon the Citroën-based, Merak-engined V6 Quattroporte II. This was never much more than a prototype, of which perhaps five were made, but De Tomaso loathed the complexity of the French designs and had supplanted it in 1977 with a traditional V8-powered luxury saloon, which became known as the Quattroporte III, though it took another two years to put into production (*see* Chapter 12).

De Tomaso saw a natural opportunity in the prestige four-door saloon market for a cheaper version of the Quattroporte, so he was quick to fill it with yet another variation on the Biturbo theme, a much more accessible four-door, but still with the Maserati cachet.

The 425 – four doors and 2.5 litres – was announced in December 1983 and introduced in 1984, though was hardly in volume production that year since only 250 or so were built. It combined the sporting aspects of the coupé with the space and convenience of a 4-door prestige saloon, not quite in the dripping decadence style of the Quattroporte tradition, but was still a high-grade competitor for the Saab 9000 and German rivals such as the Audi Quattro, the BMW 3 Series and the Mercedes 190 2.3-16.

Floor plan stretched

To accommodate the extra space the coupé floor pan was stretched so that it was 9.72in (24.7mm) longer and 3.38in (8.58mm) was added to the wheelbase. It was also just over half an inch (16mm) wider. The height was increased slightly to allow for headroom in the rear seats. It was now larger than the BMW 3 Series, but about the same length as a Ford Sierra.

The engine and suspension were largely standard 2.5 Biturbo, though power was 203bhp at 5,500rpm compared with the coupe's 185bhp. The body was not just a quick re-skin of the coupé – every body panel from the engine bulkhead to the tail was different. Inside there was Missoni patterned velour upholstery or there was leather, which was standard for US cars, as was power steering and three-speed automatic transmission. Central locking appeared for the first time.

American buyers paid a relatively high price: in May 1986 when it was tested by *Car and Driver* the 425 cost $31,270 including the gas-guzzler tax that had now soared to $1,500; adding the optional intercooler kit would add another $1,500. Most of its competitors, such as the BMW, cost less, though cars like the Mercedes 190 2.3-16 and the Jaguar XJ6 were between 3,000 and 4,000 dollars more than the 425's base price.

There was high praise for the luxurious interior, none at all for the bucking and stalling before it had warmed up, something that nearly all the road tests of the carburetted cars were to mention. The testers made the point, which applied also to the coupé, that performance from rest was very slow until the turbos kicked in at 3,500rpm and the car took off; until then they claimed to have been overtaken by mopeds and even bicycles. But rocket travel came at a price – overall consumption was 13mpg in the city and 15mpg on the highway, not quite

Testing the 425

This Maserati 425 was one of the very first officially imported to the UK in 1986, costing a heady £27,795 (more than an Audi quattro) and was used for the *Motor's* road test. John Simister, who did the testing, recalled it twenty years later as a fairly terrible car:

> In the wet its handling teetered between heavy understeer and power oversteer, the latter difficult to meter because of the imprecise throttle response and ample turbo boost, and its fuel consumption was disastrously bad: a test average of 15.5mpg.
>
> The handbrake was hopeless and there were lots of detail finish and assembly faults. It's not as if it was a brand new design with teething troubles, because Maserati had been making Biturbos for six years by the time I wrote that test.
>
> After the test had gone to press, the 425 developed another fault. It would build up massive amounts of boost with the gauge's needle jammed against the end of the scale, accelerating like nothing on earth and detonating copiously as it did so. I guess the wastegate was sticking shut. Anyway, it held together and that's how it went back to Maserati's new UK importer.

The pictures were taken by Maurice Rowe alongside the airship hangers at Cardington, in Bedfordshire, where the ill-fated R101 was built. (LAT)

as bad as it sounds as the US gallon is 0.83 of a British gallon.

Despite the initial hesitation in getting off the mark, the 0–60mph time was a useful 7.9sec, though maximum speed at 122mph (196km/h) was well below Maserati claims and European tests. This was probably due to the emissions equipment as well as the extra weight. *Car*'s continental test in September 1984 said that despite its more matronly lines – and a 200lb (90kg) weight penalty compared with the coupé – the 425's performance was nearly as good as that of the the new Biturbo S. Without the strangling US emissions equipment it got from 0–60mph in 6.5sec. But in handling terms, it was clearly meant for long autobahn hauls than for quick dashes across mountain passes.

The first British test of the 425 was reported in *Performance Car* in July 1986; it was in a privately owned, left-hand-drive car as right-hand-drive cars were still imported though they began to be made from that year. They loved the performance, but hated the inside with its Fiat air vents, and leatherette and suede in different colours and textures. If you were used to BMWs or Jaguars 'the Missoni interior will offend your eye, though some may call it Italian flair and cover a multitude of sins'.

'The Missoni interiors were hideous in blue and some in burnt orange', recalled Anthony Cazalet of the cars that were finally imported into the UK, 'we could scarcely give the cars away.'

On the road, said *Performance Car*, if you forgave the low-speed snatch, it excelled. At the red line of 6,500rpm it was just under the motorway limit of 70mph in only second gear. 'Third gear acceleration brings back memories of M635s and much more expensive exotica.' It offered an excellent engine, allied to a fair transmission and a balanced chassis.

425 four-door saloon (1984–87)

Engine	
Type	AM453
Layout	V6 90 degrees – 3 valves per cylinder, single overhead cam per bank, two IHI turbochargers
Bore × stroke:	91.6 × 63mm
Capacity:	2491cc
Compression ratio:	7.8:1
Max power:	196bhp/146.2kW@5,600rpm
Max torque:	205lb ft/28.34kg m@3,600rpm
Fuel system:	Weber twin-choke carburettor
Intercoolers:	None
Transmission	
Gearbox:	ZF manual 5 speed + reverse. Automatic 3-speed option
Final drive:	Sensitork 3.31:1
Suspension	
Front:	MacPherson strut with anti-roll bar, coil springs, shock absorbers
Rear:	Trailing arms, coil springs, shock absorbers, anti-roll bar
Steering:	Power-assisted rack and pinion
Brakes:	Servo-assisted twin circuit, front and rear ventilated discs with floating calipers, rear drum parking brake.
Running gear	
Wheels:	6½J × 14
Tyres:	205/60VR14
Performance	
Max speed:	140mph (225km/h)
Acceleration:	0–62mph (100km/h) in 6.6sec
Dimensions	
Wheelbase:	102.4in (2,600mm)
Front track:	56.8in (1,442mm)
Rear track:	57.2in (1,453mm)
Length:	173.2in (4,400mm)
Width:	68.1in (1,730mm)
Height:	53.6in (1,360mm)
Weight:	2,600lb (1,180kg)
Number built	2,372

The clock

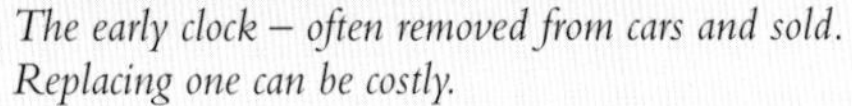
The early clock – often removed from cars and sold. Replacing one can be costly.

The latest version in the Maserati GranSport.

'A classic gold Swiss clock floats on the rosewood facia keeping perfect time.' Maserati UK brochure 1989

Maserati road cars have had their familiar oval clock on the dashboard for many years. It has been fitted as standard, on other occasions it has been made an option, as it is in the 2005 US-specification Spyder Cambiocorsa, at a cost of $210.

It didn't appear at all in the Quattroporte evoluzione of 1998, as Maserati's new owners, Ferrari, thought it smacked too much of the De Tomaso era and substituted in its traditional place a trident badge on a piece of veneer. Drivers had to make do with a cheap-looking digital clock near the gear lever. However, the 2005 Quattroporte and the other contemporary models have the oval timepiece fitted again, but rather than the gold of the 1980s it is now in a more tasteful silver surround with a blue dial.

Over the years, clock faces have been gold, white and blue; the oval surrounds have been gold, silver or, more recently, brushed aluminium.

The Maserati clocks were named after a master watchmaker, Jean Lassale of Geneva, who, in 1976, created the thinnest movement ever made for a wristwatch. The early clocks were marked Lasalle and made in Switzerland, not by watchmaker Jean hunched over a bench but by the giant Japanese Seiko Group, to whom he sold out in the 1980s. Early clocks were powered by a small 1.55-volt silver oxide battery and the clock had to be taken out of the facia to replace it, with the risk of damaging the veneer. Later versions were powered directly from the electrical system.

In 1988, Maserati took a full page in *Autocar* trumpeting the virtues of the 2.5, but almost half the copy revolved around the clock, which it used as a device to flatter the ego of the potential customer:

> ... and then there's the clock. An expensive gold Swiss clock. It symbolizes our philosophy perfectly – Old World, but not old-fashioned. It allows us to take advantage of technical advance without forgetting that you're foremost a driver, not an engineer.

> And recognizing that you judge a car by its comfort, style and performance, not simply by its technological accompaniments. (In short, you wouldn't have a digital clock in your lounge, so why suffer one in the car?)

The clock, it has to be said, is not to everyone's taste, though many have been removed from Maserati dashes to be used in houses; buying one second-hand is not cheap. It even appears in the road-going version of the fearsome MC 12, just above the blue 'Start' button, but with a 0–60mph time of 3.7sec there isn't much time to look at it.

Road tests of various Maseratis in motoring publications have produced the following comments on the works of M. Lasalle, ranging from dismissive to highly pompous:

> 'Amusingly antique …'
> 'A gothic shape which looks rather strange in its modern surrounds …'
> 'More resembles bed-side tableware than a dash fitting …'
> 'More appropriate for your mantelpiece than a 150mph sports car.'
> 'Dominating the fascia is the most kitsch object on any modern car … after the style of Salvador Dali which looks as if is about to melt and slide down on to the carpet.'
> 'This ghastly object should be gracing the marble fireplace of some Vatican banquet hall, but it's standard equipment in all current Maseratis.'
> 'The single gimcrack in this cosy cockpit is a ridiculous jewel-like clock; it looks as if milady has Krazy Glued her 24-karat Piaget to the dash.'
> 'It is … the moral equivalent of a diamond pinky ring.'
> 'Probably the Biturbo's most reliable component.'

And from the late, orotund L. J. K. Setright:

> [It is] shaped like the vesica piscis, the ancient shape formed by the intersection of two circles, related geometrically to snowflakes and the star of David and that intriguing little Berkshire 'castle' where Edward VII made his abdication speech …'

It also tells the time.

Worth the wait?

When the Biturbo finally reached British shores in early 1987, *Motor* was moved to ask: had it been worth the wait? The 425 was priced at £24,670, which was £4,500 more than a BMW M535i and £3,000 more than the Mercedes 190 2.3-16. Leather trim was an extra £1,500 and with other extras the car as tested was a shade under £30,000. A Lotus Excel SE was nearly £10,000 cheaper.

Motor argued that rather than price-judging the 425 alongside its German competitors, it should be regarded as a four-door supercar, a cheaper alternative to Ferrari's Mondial 3.2, which was £41,250. But then it spoiled the argument by declaring that the 425 was not fast enough to be a real supercar anyway.

Blasted around the high-speed bowl at the Millbrook testing ground, where this author has also had the pleasure of taking Maseratis to the limit, the 425 reached 131.7mph (211.9km/h) in fourth, well below Maserati's claims of a 143mph (230km/h) top speed, and only 127.3mph (204.8kph) in fifth. The 0–62mph (100km/h) speed was also well short of the factory claim of 6.6sec. The engine responded with vigour above 3,000rpm and there was no uncouth rush of power or lag in throttle response as it wound its way up to a torque peak of 4,000rpm.

Inside, there were electric front seats and the optional leather and walnut oozed opulence, according to *Motor*, though no-one much liked the Beige Nuvolato orangey trim. The test car was exotic, luxurious and exclusive, but too expensive, marred by disastrous fuel consumption (15.5mpg overall), indifferent wet-weather road holding and 'a host of detail flaws'. And in addition there were no electric mirrors, variable speed wipe, trip computer or cruise control.

The magazine's final verdict, 'It's a valiant effort, but it's not for us', must have been devastating for the new importers. After all, the UK had waited years for the Biturbo to be imported officially, yet here it was being dismissed as being just not good enough.

Motor was being curmudgeonly about the level of equipment. The British version of the 425 was handsomely furnished compared with many cars of its era – as well as the electric front seats, air conditioning was standard, as were electric windows, tinted glass, hand-sewn upholstery, central locking.

Nevertheless, being a relatively small manufacturer, De Tomaso did not have the resources to upgrade continually the specification of his cars quite as quickly as Jaguar or his German competitors, and the 425 in early 1987 was still using a Weber carburettor rather than fuel injection, which it was to receive later in the year.

Anthony Cazalet recalls that there was also a design fault with the right-hand driver's door, which did not fit properly and was very difficult to close. This, of course, was less of a problem in left-hand-drive markets, which is why it took so long to resolve.

The 420 and 425 were handsome cars, with echoes of the Quattroporte. They were nearly 10in (250mm) longer than the coupé on which they were based. This is one of the first 420s. (Fonte Archivio Maserati)

It should also be mentioned that some cars hung around the dealers' showrooms for a very long time, so outdated versions were sometimes still unregistered. Few Maseratis though hung around unsold as long as a 1979 Merak which eventually found a buyer in London in 1983.

A 425 appeared in the 1989 James Bond film *Licence to Kill*.

The 420 range

Tax laws dictated that when the four-door saloon appeared in Italy during 1985 as the 420,

420/422/4.18v/4.24v four-door saloon (1985–92)

Engine	
Type	AM452.11 (420) AM470 (420i) AM471 (420Si, 422, 4.18v) AM475 (4.24v)
Layout	V6 90 degrees – 3 valves per cylinder, single overhead cam per bank; 4 valves per cylinder, double overhead cam (4.24v) Two IHI turbochargers
Bore × stroke:	82 × 63.5mm
Capacity:	1996cc
Compression ratio:	7.8:1; 7.6:1 (4.24v)
Max power:	185bhp/138kW@6,000rpm (420) 223bhp/166kW@6,250rpm (422, 4.18v) 245bhp/180kW@6,200rpm (4.24v)
Max torque:	190lb ft/26.3kg m@3,500rpm (420) 193lb ft/26.7kg m@3,500rpm (422, 4.18v) 214lb ft/29.6kg m@3,500rpm (4.24v)
Fuel system:	Weber twin-choke carburettor (420); injection (422, 4.18v, 4.24v)
Intercoolers:	None (420, 422); two air-to-air (4.18v, 4.24v)
Transmission	
Gearbox:	ZF manual 5 speed + reverse, automatic 3-speed option
Final drive:	Sensitork 3.7:1; Ranger 3.73:1 (4.24v)

Suspension	
Front:	MacPherson strut with anti-roll bar, coil springs, shock absorbers.
Rear:	Trailing arms, coil springs, shock absorbers, anti-roll bar
Steering:	Power-assisted rack and pinion
Brakes:	Servo-assisted twin circuit, front and rear ventilated discs with floating calipers, rear drum parking brake.
Running gear	
Wheels:	$6\frac{1}{2}$J × 14; 7J × 16 (4.24v)
Tyres:	205/60VR14 (420) 205/55VR14 (4.18v) 205/45 R16 85Z (4.24v)
Max speed	136mph (220km/h) to 142mph (230km/h)

Dimensions	420	4.24v
Wheelbase:	102.4in (2,600mm)	99.0in (2,514mm)
Front track:	56.8in (1,442mm)	57.4in (1,458mm)
Rear track:	57.2in (1,453mm)	57.2in (1,454mm)
Length:	173.2in (4,400mm)	
Width:	68.1in (1,730mm)	
Height:	53.6in (1,360mm)	53.9in (1,370mm)
Weight:	2,600lb (1,180kg)	3,020lb (1,370kg)
Number built	6,151	

Marketing Maseratis

America was – and still is – the most important export market for Maserati. According to *Automotive News* in 2005, the fourth year since its return to North America, sales boomed from 917 in 2003 to 1,043 in 2004 and double that figure in 2005; more than 70 per cent of these were Quattroportes.

At the height of Biturbo exports in the 1980s, there were sixty-eight dealers in the USA, fourteen of them in California alone. Compare that with the UK network in the 1970s and 1980s, which ranged from four to a dozen or so.

The Biturbo was imported into the east coast of America by Maserati Automobiles Inc. at Caton Avenue, Baltimore, Maryland, which also housed the parts facility. The company was owned jointly by De Tomaso and Norwegian-born Kjell Qvale, who had had a close relationship with De Tomaso since ordering 250 Mangustas from De Tomaso Automobili in the late 1960s.

'The Mangusta benefited from a fascinating and beautiful design, but adequate testing could have cured the mechanical flaws', Qvale wrote in his autobiography. 'This shortcoming on the part of De Tomaso was evident in varying degrees in all the cars he produced both before and after the Mangusta.' And of course with the Biturbo.

Qvale had handled mainly British imports and had been heavily involved in trying to revive Jensen in Britain, but when De Tomaso took over Maserati, Qvale was given the US distribution rights for the eleven western states through the Maserati Import Co. in Van Ness Avenue, San Francisco. The distribution centre was in Los Angeles. This was one of his many companies, including British Motors, which is still there.

By the time the Biturbo went on sale in America, Qvale had become chairman of the board of De Tomaso Industries, holding 10 per cent of the stock and thus indirectly owning part of Maserati.

When interviewed by *Car and Driver*, he described De Tomaso, perhaps unsurprisingly, as a genius; as to the Biturbo it was a 'magnificent machine, worthy of the history of Maserati' and the most exciting car of its type that he had ever driven. This closeness was to end some years later in bitter recriminations.

Qvale had become involved in the UK when he tried to save the West Midlands car maker Jensen, whose cars he sold in the USA, but it collapsed under the weight of the oil crisis and dire industrial relations. What was salvaged from the wreckage was the service and spares backup for Jensen, which became part of a company called International Motors. It was an offshoot of this firm, called Modena Concessionaires and set up by Qvale, that took on the task of importing and selling Maseratis.

The import of Maseratis in the 1960s and 1970s into the UK before Modena Concessionaires is rather a tangled tale. In the 1960s there was the Chipstead Group, then MTC cars, in Holland Park Mews, West London. MTC was named after Mario Tozzi-Condivi, Italian entrepreneur, former Rolls-Royce salesman and first major importer of BMWs into the UK. In 1977, now retailing Maseratis, Alfas and De Tomaso's own cars, MTC moved to lavish premises in Beavor Lane, Hammersmith, West London.

MTC, in turn, were supplied through the Channel Islands by a company called Maserati Right-Hand Drive Ltd which, as its name suggests, handled the distribution in all right-hand-drive markets, including Australia. But none of the cars ever went near Channel Islands as it was a paper company designed to build in another profit margin.

Behind this company was the same Tozzi-Condivi ('Maserati is almost a second religion to me'), an old friend of de Tomaso's, who later became president of Moto-Guzzi.

When MTC ran into difficulties in 1980, Modena Concessionaires took over. This was part of the rump of the old Jensen company, which had gone into receivership. It was based in West Bromwich and was run by Robert Edmiston, an accountant who had worked for Ford and Chrysler and who had become Qvale's finance director at Jensen.

Over a period of years, he bought the entire stake from Qvale and transformed it into the International Motors Group, which still holds the immensely profitable British franchise for Subaru, Daihatsu and Isuzu. His personal wealth was said by the *Sunday Times* in 2005 to be £325m – in 2004 he gave £27m to Christian Vision.

Modena Concessionaires handled the import of the Maserati Kyalami, Khamsin and Merak as well as De Tomaso's own cars like the Pantera. 'We had a legal suit for every De Tomaso we sold and the Maseratis were not very reliable either', recalled Edmiston in an interview with the author. 'We got stuck with a lot of them and could not get the newer models.'

BITURBO

NEGATIVE No. B66-1b

OCTOBER 1982

The hopeful British importer, International Motors, put out this publicity shot in the UK in October 1982. It is evidently a left-hand-drive car because of the position of the driving mirror, and few Biturbos had been built at this stage. It was to be another four years before right-hand-drive cars were made, by which time International Motors had given up the franchise. (I.M. Group Ltd)

The pre-Biturbo Maseratis were going out of production and in 1982–3 Modena sold only seventy-eight cars; the continuing delays in providing a right-hand-drive Biturbo infuriated Edmiston who, to De Tomaso's great displeasure, compared Maserati's reliability to that of a jobbing builder. De Tomaso riposted in a letter that Edmiston was a 'salami and mortadella salesman', though this was translated by Tozzi-Condivi for a solicitor's letter as 'a fish and chip salesman'.

'What is most upsetting', Edmiston was reported as saying at the time, 'is that if we don't keep on with Maserati, it will be the only branch of the business that has failed'. Eventually, they did abandon the franchise in September 1985. Recalling the events twenty years later, Edmiston said:

> It was a bit of a disaster and the termination was mutual. We could not get along with De Tomaso; he had very skilled people but not a lot of resources and an unwillingness to invest. And then there was the quality issue. We went to the factory once and said to them, 'Look at this area in the Biturbo, rust will develop here', but they would not do anything about it.

continued overleaf

Marketing Maseratis *continued*

Since there was no right-hand-drive model, De Tomaso pressed Edmiston to sell left-hand-drive cars in Britain instead, which met with a dusty answer:

> We asked him to give us a Biturbo to exhibit at the London motor show. The model he sent us was an engineering car, which must have had 5,000–10,000km on the clock. It was dented and rusty. He said it was a new car; I told him it was a disgrace and we sent it back, but he made us pay for it. It was a crazy attitude to marketing a car.

International Motors' technical staff who worked there at the time recalled two cars coming from Modena with the paint peeling off them in sheets, probably because it had been applied to dirty surfaces. Exit Modena Concessionaires.

When the Biturbo officially reached Britain in 1986, it was marketed by a new company, Maserati (UK) Ltd, under the chairmanship of the ubiquitous Mario Tozzi-Condivi, a close friend of Aurelio Bertocchi, who had persuaded him to fill the vacuum in Britain. It was announced that there would soon be thirty dealers in the UK (again) and that Maserati was aiming to take 2 per cent of the 'fine car' market.

At this time Maserati UK's headquarters were in offices rented by the day in Kensington High Street, London. Anthony Cazalet, who was then the company's technical director, recalled:

> We were a shoestring operation. The big problem that we had was that in March 1986 the Italian lira was 3,000 to the pound and by the time the cars arrived at the end of the year the rate was 2,000 to the pound. For every 100 lira it went down we had to increase the price in England by £1,000. In March we thought we would be able to sell the coupé for £17,500, but the reality was £25,000.

Despite the shortage of money, there was a lavish party with Fangio and Moss present when a new showroom was opened at James Young in Berkeley Street, Mayfair, on 14 April 1987. In July of that year, there were twenty-one dealers in the UK. The coupé was selling at £24,795, the 425 at £27,795 and the Spyder at £28,795 and Maserati UK were promising, according to *Autocar*, a 24-month warranty and a six-year anti-rust guarantee. The company soon ran into difficulties and, after selling a total of ninety-nine carburetted cars, the business was sold in September 1987 to a consortium of businessmen in the north of England.

The new owners set up shop with a staff of twenty on an unlikely site for a prestige car importer: an industrial estate in Leeds, near Elland Road football ground. The new managing director, Nick May, announced that the 18,000sq ft base in Leeds would act as a dealership and import centre. The chairman by now was John Bogg; on his death in January 1989, his executors sold it to another of his former companies, Hekla Holdings, based in Hull, which also marketed caravans and trailers – unlikely companions for a prestige car operation.

Maserati's time in the UK during the De Tomaso era was characterized by exceedingly optimistic estimates of cars that would be sold through a much-enlarged dealer network. Predictions in 1987 had been for 400 Biturbos a year to be sold through thirty new dealers in Britain. These sales never materialized.

For 1988, the new managing director of Maserati (UK), Michael Blakey, was hoping to sell between 250–350 cars. 'The old company did not have the money to support the dealers properly', he was quoted as saying. 'We have.' In fact, Maserati sales in the UK in 1988 were 145, mainly the 2.8 cars, and in 1989 they were 151. By that time the dealer network was down to eighteen, as many had been weeded out.

Luigi Maraffi, an ex-Alfa man who was the Maserati UK sales manager at the time, says that although there were more than twenty dealers in the UK, a few of them were discounting the cars to make sales, which weakened the brand. He was also perturbed by the cloth interiors of some of the cars – 'they were dreadful, the colours were awful' – but had little difficulty selling the cars generally, as the ordering was done very carefully.

At the end of the 1980s, the executive running the franchise, Stan Cholaj, who had previously been at Ford and Nissan, issued a new prediction: Maserati sales increasing to 250 or more in 1991 and doubling the following year. The dealer network was now down to twelve – though well up from the four of 1977 – and was to be expanded to twenty.

'Hekla Holdings seems to have the financial clout to make a success of the marque', declared *Performance Car* in

October 1990. They could not have been more wrong. Hekla slid into receivership shortly afterwards, many millions of pounds seem to have disappeared and a messy High Court case ensued.

For a time, the franchise was being run from a shed on Dover docks and it emerged from the ashes when Meridien Motors of Lyndhurst and Bournemouth, run by the Butt family, bought it out of receivership in 1991, with the entire stock of vehicles, parts and administration records. Meridian Modena Concessionaires Ltd was formed in January 1992. The Butt family opened up with forty-nine new Maseratis, according to the motoring magazines – 228s, Spyders, 430s and 222s – and £½m in parts. They ran it as the sole Maserati concessionaire for the UK until 1998, when the Ferrari UK importer, Maranello Concessionaires, part of the Inchcape group, took it over, a move linked to Ferrari's acquisition of Maserati in June 1997.

Meridien still sell Maseratis at a dealership in lavish showrooms at Lyndhurst in the New Forest, originally built as the Imperial Motor Works in the 1920s. Inchcape sell Maseratis and Ferraris through dealerships in Egham, St Albans and Sevenoaks. In October 2004, when Maserati moved out of the financial grasp of Ferrari, the franchise reverted to the factory and the British headquarters is now in Slough. Ferrari Maserati UK took over the import and distribution activities, which had been managed by Maranello Concessionaires Ltd. Finally, in March 2006 the name became Maserati GB Ltd.

The American import and parts operation in Baltimore closed in December 1994. No more cars were being imported, as reliability and service issues had forced Maserati to leave the American market in 1991. The parts division was bought by MIE Corp, the commercial arm of the Maserati Club International, which now operates from Seattle. The building in Caton Avenue became a Toyota service depot.

Maserati itself returned to the American market in January 2002 with the 4200 coupé.

it was powered by the 2.0-litre, carburetted version of the Biturbo engine, which put out 185bhp. It proved very popular and nearly 3,000 were sold within a year. In 1986, a fuel injection version was introduced and the car became the 420i.

The following year a faster version, the 420Si, appeared. It was again for the Italian market and had an extra 35bhp. It had fuel injection, water-cooled turbos and an air-to-air intercooler fed through NACA bonnet ducts. An opening sun roof was also a feature.

In 1988, yet another 2.0-litre four-door version for Italy appeared; this was the 422, which looked like a 430 (*see* Chapter 7) externally and had the same running gear.

The only difference was the smaller engine: it had the V6 with two turbochargers and two air-to-air intercoolers, active mechanical suspension and the 430's 'Ranger' differential. The NACA ducts on the bonnet were deleted.

The 4.18v

The 422 was updated in 1990 with the appearance of the 4.18v – for eighteen valves – which had similar performance to the 422, with 223bhp at 6,250rpm. This version of the Biturbo had ABS brakes at last.

Then, finally in this four-door, 2.0-litre class came the four-valve engine in the 4.24v – for twenty-four valves – which developed 245bhp at 6,200rpm.

(Fonte Archivio Maserati)

6 The Chryslerati – the Maserati TC

> Those who shape the limited edition sport coupés that Maserati is building for Chrysler are prideful people who have always built their automobiles as if each were one of a kind.
>
> *Chrysler television advertisement*

American car makers seem fatally drawn to investing in European motor manufacturers and then incurring huge losses. This syndrome has continued well into the new millennium, with Ford in 2006 looking at a $327 million deficit on their prestige car group of Jaguar, Aston Martin and so on. General Motors signed a deal in 2000 to take 20 per cent of Fiat Auto, with an option to buy the whole company, which went spectacularly wrong, costing GM billions of dollars.

Chrysler, now part of DaimlerChrysler, have avoided this European black hole by successfully producing from 1993 the Jeep Grand Cherokee at the Steyr-Daimler-Puch plant in Graz, Austria. They were not always as lucky: in July 1964 Chrysler bought two failing European car makers, the Rootes group (Humber, Hillman, Singer and Sunbeam) in England and the Simca concern in France, combining them into Chrysler Europe. Chrysler were not to be much more successful than Ford or GM, gratefully retreating to America and abandoning the group to Peugeot in 1978.

Which made it all the more remarkable that as the Biturbo production was building up in 1984, the Chrysler Corporation paid $2.3m for a 3.47 per cent stake in Maserati, that valued a company, which was on its knees a few years previously, at many millions. By 1986 the stake was up to 15.6 per cent and there was talk of making it 51 per cent within eight years with the options that Chrysler had got.

Plans began to be developed for a Chrysler grand tourer with European credentials, built in Italy for the American market, which would add lustre to the somewhat pedestrian range of K-cars launched in 1981, originally as the Plymouth Reliant and Dodge Aries – six-seater, front-wheel-drive cars – launched to fight off the Japanese invasion.

Dull they might have been, but they and their Minivan derivative saved Chrysler from financial disaster. One later upmarket version of the K range was the Chrysler LeBaron, available in both saloon and convertible form, and this turned out to be remarkably like 'The Chrysler TC by Maserati' as it was eventually styled – a two-seater, front-wheel-drive convertible.

Crucial to the scheme was the close, twenty-year relationship between the buccaneering Alejandro De Tomaso and the brash chairman of Chrysler, Lee Iacocca, who oversaw the K-series into production, though he did not originate it. They had worked closely together before when Iacocca, the marketing genius behind the Mustang, was president at Ford and Henry Ford II was casting about in the 1960s for an Italian car firm to buy – to please his wife, it was said, who was herself Italian. He had tried Ferrari, then Lancia, and had been rebuffed by both.

Ford engines

But De Tomaso, who was already using Ford engines in his own cars, had no such scruples. For $5m he sold Ford his Ghia and Vignale

The porthole in the glassfibre hardtop was a Detroit styling gimmick going back to the 1956 Ford Thunderbird, though some claimed it allowed vision in the rear three-quarter blind spot. (DaimlerChrysler Corporation)

coachbuilding firms, then a chunk of his own company on the understanding that Iacocca would market his new Ford-engined, Ghia-bodied Pantera in America through Lincoln Mercury dealers. Thousands were produced from 1971, but they were not well built, they rusted and they were not sufficiently adapted for the American market. It was said that Ford was having to pay an average of $1,800 per car to have faults rectified, so the relationship ended sourly in 1974.

Ford fired Iacocca in 1978. He went to Chrysler and with his old friend De Tomaso produced the following year the Dodge Omni De Tomaso 024 – a lacklustre, VW-engined, front-wheel-drive car tricked out for this special edition with spoilers, flared wheel arches and sports suspension. It cost an extra $1,575.

'From his shop in Modena, Italy, Alejandro De Tomaso has produced a dramatic optional package … truly worthy of the name he made famous', ran the hype. Needless to say the car had been nowhere near Italy, as the modifications were made by a firm in Detroit.

This is relevant to the Maserati story because it shows how Iacocca was a master at gilding the lily, and what was to happen next was an attempt to attach the considerable prestige of Maserati to a mid-range American convertible and charge people a great deal of money for the privilege. And what was in it for Maserati? A lucrative contract and bagfuls of dollars to update De Tomaso's Milan works, which were producing real Maseratis.

'More than decade and a half has passed since Lee Iacocca an Alejandro De Tomaso first spoke of building a sport car (sic) together', burbled the first brochure. 'It became a reality only after these two inveterate experimenters had meticulously critiqued a new car into existence.' It called the TC a life-quickening automobile with 'a heritage that melds sixty years of Chrysler engineering leadership with seventy years of Maserati coachbuilding mastery.'

Chrysler were aiming the car at the luxury sports car market in America, dominated by the Mercedes SL, but about to be entered by General Motors with the Cadillac Allanté – another two-seater, front-wheel-drive convertible with an Italian heritage, but retailing at more than $50,000 compared with the $30,000 or so that was to be asked for the TC.

Seemingly undeterred by the Pantera's misfortunes in the USA, Iacocca was ready by 1984 for this new Italian venture. Chrysler and Maserati announced their joint project, the Q-coupé. Not a coupé at all, but a soft-top with an occasional glassfibre hardtop, adorned with 1950s Ford Thunderbird-type portholes. These had what was called the Pentatrident symbol in the glass – the Trident emblem enclosed in the Chrysler pentastar.

Autocar in Britain had pictures of the prototype car in November 1985. Production was scheduled for late 1986, it reported.

The 'best-looking Italian'

'This could well be the best-looking Italian to show up in America since my mother came over', declared the ebullient Iacocca as he introduced the prototype to Chrysler dealers in 1985. Less publicly, he referred to it as the Chryslerati.

Externally, the Maserati influence was nowhere to be seen. The body was designed at Chrysler headquarters at Highland Park, Michigan, and the prototype was built in California. The chassis was to be a version of the K-series, whose sheet metal was shipped over to Italy. The suspension, steering and air conditioning also came from America, as did minor parts like instrument clusters and door handles. The soft top came from Michigan, the hard top from Germany, the bumper extrusions from Norway, the tyres from Michelin from France, the wiring loom came from Barcelona and the ABS brakes were by the German firm Teves.

Italian thoroughbred it was not, but then neither is the 2005 Aston Martin V8 Vantage a truly British sports car – the engine is made by Ford in Cologne, body parts come from Norway and France and the gearbox from Italy.

Testing of the TC was done at MIRA in England – 667 laps of a 1.5-mile (3.2km) rough Belgian pavé track – and on a frozen lake in Sweden.

The engines

There were to be two launch engines. The first, the familiar 2.2-litre, four-cylinder, single overhead cam turbocharged unit from the Dodge Daytona, was shipped over from America, complete with transaxle, but the cylinder head was cast in Italy by a Fiat subsidiary. This engine was Chrysler's first metric power plant introduced in 1981; the normally aspirated version put out 96bhp at 5,200rpm, but the Turbo II version with intercooler in the TC produced 160bhp at 5,200rpm. This engine was offered in 1989 only.

The Maserati connection came with another four-cylinder option: a hotter sixteen-valve, aluminium double overhead camshaft head on the Chrysler block. On the cam covers it proclaimed 'CHRYSLER by Maserati'. Designing the head had involved three sets of engineers: Chrysler, Lotus and Maserati. The Maserati design was chosen and then its aluminium casting was farmed out to Cosworth in England for fabrication. The head was 'finished' by Maserati in Italy; the pistons were German, by Mahle.

This twin-cam developed 220lb ft of torque at 5,500rpm and 200bhp at 5,500rpm, which Chrysler claimed could get the 3,000lb (1,360kg) car to 135mph (217km/h) and sprint from 0–60mph in 8sec; in fact, *Road and Track* managed it in 6.9sec. This dohc head is often confused with a similar one that Chrysler used on the same block in 1991, which was Lotus-designed and used in the Dodge Spirit and Daytona.

There was to be a third engine in the last two years of production, a 141bhp, 3-litre Mitsubishi V6 seen in many Chrysler cars. Mitsubishi had been involved with Chrysler on joint ventures since 1970 when Chrysler bought 35 per cent of the company and in

Chrysler TC by Maserati (1988–89)

Engine	
Type:	Chrysler R2.2T
Layout:	Transverse inline 4, 16-valve, double overhead cam Maserati head, IHI turbo
Bore × stroke:	87.5 × 92 mm
Capacity:	2213cc
Compression ratio:	7.3:1
Max power:	200bhp/149.1kW@5,500rpm
Max torque:	220lb ft/30.4kg m@3,400rpm
Fuel system:	Holley electronic fuel injection
Intercooler:	one air-to-air
Transmission	
Gearbox:	Getrag manual 5 speed + reverse
Final drive:	Front-wheel drive
Suspension	
Front:	Fichtel and Sachs gas-charged Isostruts
Rear:	Trailing beam axle, coil springs, arms, coil springs, gas struts
Steering:	Power-assisted rack and pinion
Brakes:	Teves servo-assisted discs, ABS
Running gear	
Wheels:	6J × 15
Tyres:	205/60VR15
Performance	
Max speed:	135mph (217km/h)
Acceleration:	0–60mph (96.5km/h) in 6.9sec
Dimensions	
Wheelbase:	92.9in (2,360mm)
Front track:	57.5in (1,460mm)
Rear track:	57.5in (1,460mm)
Length:	175.8in (4,465mm)
Width:	68.5in (1,740mm)
Height:	52in (1,320mm)
Weight:	3,090lb (1,400kg)
Number built	501

1988 had begun production in a joint corporation, Diamond Star Motors in Bloomington, Illinois, which turned out cars such as the Plymouth Laser, Eagle Talon and Mitsubishi Eclipse. More TCs were made with this Japanese V6 engine, which put out 141bhp at 5,000rpm, than any of the others, as they accounted for nearly 50 per cent of production.

The single cam engine was fitted with the Chrysler three-speed auto A413 TorqueFlite transaxle, with a final drive ratio of 3.02:1. The Maserati version had a German Getrag five-speed manual box, with synchromesh on reverse; some 500 of these were made. Then for the Mitsubishi engine there was a four-speed auto Ultradrive.

Hand-assembly

The final hand-assembly was by workers paid half the rate of their American counterparts. In charge of the project for Maserati was none other than De Tomaso's son Santiago, today the keeper of his father's flame.

Despite all the major components being American – some estimates say that as many as 1,200 parts were from the USA – it was maintained officially that 75 per cent of the content was Italian. However, in the opaque language of the car industry this means not just parts, but all labour costs and overheads, down to the subsidizing of the pasta in the works canteen.

Chrysler produced a brochure for dealers and stockholders promoting the SC – the 'Sport Coupe Built by Maserati'. The select group of Chrysler dealers chosen to market the car in America was told to expect a launch date of spring 1987. In fact, all that happened that spring was that in April Chrysler ventured even further into the uncertain world of Italian motor manufacturing by buying 100 per cent of Lamborghini. (They sold out in 1994 to an Indonesian group.)

There had been much euphoria after the car's announcement. *Car and Driver* declared after Iacocca's presentation:

> It's a new way of doing business in Detroit; move fast, strike with the sharp end of the stick and catch the competition with their drawers on the floor. Chrysler and Maserati are using their best resources – their brains – to tool up a high-impact machine that the public won't soon forget.

Alas, moving fast was the last thing that happened; Maserati had promised production and no car appeared in 1987 other than two that were used as pace cars for the grand prix at Monte Carlo.

It didn't appear in 1988 either, though by now the publicity was calling it the TC – 'Chrysler's Turbo Convertible Built by Maserati', which gave specifications for the sixteen-valve 'Maserati' engine. There was thought at one stage of calling it the Lido – Iacocca's real first name.

The continuing delays became a joke in the industry as planned launches were cancelled because of 'technical difficulties'. This was hurting Chrysler's reputation, and in addition Iacocca's new luxury Imperial model bombed and the new Spirit and Acclaim models got a very poor reception – Chrysler's engineers referred to people who bought them as PODS (poor, old, dumb shits), according to Doron Levin's book on Iacocca.

Lurching towards a launch

'Still awaiting introduction by Chrysler is the Chrysler by Alfieri Maserati Automobil (sic) sports import', reported *Ward's Auto World* in August 1987. 'Around 100 of the luxury units are expected from Italy in October, rising to 400 monthly by December and 600 monthly in early '88.'

But by October *Ward's* was reporting, 'Chrysler Motors Corp. still is lurching toward a formal 'final' launch of its pricey Maserati TC convertible, but no official introduction date has been set.'

It was evident by early 1998 that De Tomaso himself had begun to realize that the TC project was becoming an embarrassment and was forced onto the defensive by journalists at a news conference about whether it was hurting Maserati's image. 'Why should it?', he was reported by *Car* magazine. 'Chrysler is doing an enormous amount to promote the car and that promotion is good for Maserati.' But then he went on testily, 'Don't ask me whether I like the TC or am happy with the car. It's not my car – ask Chrysler.'

This seems rather ungracious, to say the least, given Chrysler's 15.6 per cent stake in Maserati, let alone the rivers of cash that they had poured into De Tomaso's manufacturing facilities. But by then the Italian dream for Chrysler had become a very expensive nightmare and in September 1988 they renounced their options to buy a majority stake in Maserati. A disappointed De Tomaso remarked tartly, 'Better alone than in the wrong company.'

Production difficulties

The lines of communication were long even when the TC components had reached Italy from Detroit and various parts of Europe. The American galvanized sheet metal for the body was first stamped at ITCA near Turin, across the road from Pininfarina's works, then welded and assembled by a firm at Sparone, 44 miles (70km) north of what the brochure insists on calling Turino. So much for Maserati coachbuilding mastery...

Then the body-in-white was off to Innocenti in Milan, for dipping in a nine-step anti-corrosion treatment and painting. The mechanics were added as was the Maserati content – the Pasubio leather interior and the mechanics.

Logistical problems were common because of the long supply chains and there had been severe problems as new workers were trained in new

TC bodies in white undergoing quality checks on the line. Activity is far from feverish. (DaimlerChrysler Corporation)

The high-quality Pasubio leather interior is delicate and prone to drying and cracking in hot American sun. (DaimlerChrysler Corporation)

techniques and paint shop problems were resolved. In addition, labour unrest, mismanagement of the project, including disputes between Chrysler and Maserati engineers, hampered the project to a degree where it was running very late: Maserati had promised the first cars by September 1986, which turned out to be hopelessly optimistic. Iacocca sent to Milan his hatchetman, Dick Dauch, who was in charge of all the Chrysler factories, to get production flowing.

By contrast, Cadillac had announced the Allanté in 1985 – the same year as the TC – and the car was on sale by 1987. The chassis was built in Detroit, shipped to Italy for its Pininfarina body, and then flown back to America in specially converted Boeing 747s for final assembly. This did not prevent several quality problems appearing, including a leaky roof.

Chrysler's project manager for the TC, Bob Davis, maintains that while Maserati's estimate of twenty-three months to get the car into production was unrealistic and known to be so, the TC's time to get into production of forty-three months was not unusual for Chrysler and actually less than the Dodge Daytona, which took forty-eight months.

After maddening delays, the first TCs came off the line in May 1988 and were shipped to Germany to be exported to America; by December 1988 they were being unloaded in California, looking somewhat different to the prototype of 1985 and rather like a slightly smaller version of the Chrysler LeBaron GTC convertible, though none of the body panels was interchangeable. The LeBaron was a $20,000 car – the TC's initial price was $33,550. Chrysler wrote to prospective customers in January 1989 offering them priority delivery if the orders were in by February.

TC drivers lacked for nothing. The car had a Haartz fabric-lined soft top with the glassfibre hardtop for bad weather. There was air-conditioning, central locking, electric tinted windows, heated exterior mirrors and an Infinity stereo. The lavishly upholstered, electrically operated leather seats were from Conceria Pasubio in Arzignano and had six-way adjustment. The CD player was originally standard, but later a dealer option.

FondMetal alloys

The wheels were splendid and very expensive 15 × 6in FondMetal alloys from the family foundry near Bergamo that made the cylinder blocks and head for the Biturbo – and still makes Formula One wheels today.

For life's little emergencies there was a zip-up leather case, which contained a Swiss Army knife, a double-ended screwdriver, first-aid bandages and tape, a tyre pressure gauge, a pair of leather gloves and a pair of pliers. If it rained, there was an umbrella held by three clips under the top of the spare tyre compartment – an idea recently revived by Rolls-Royce, though theirs are in the doors. The toolkit and umbrella were put in the cars when they arrived in the USA, but many cars had one or the other item missing.

There were five basic body colours: Royal Cabernet, Exotic Red, Light Yellow, Jet Black and Arctic White. Smoke Quartz was catalogued but not offered, though a car has subsequently been painted in this colour. The interior trim could be had in Black, Ginger or Bordeaux. Chrysler's television ads in America lauded the 'hand-crafted European coachwork' and the 'sea of soft leather'.

A book published in 2004 entitled *Automotive Atrocities* included both the TC and the Biturbo in its 'loathsome luxury' section. But then, since it included in another section two of the most successful European cars of the twentieth century, the Citroën 2CV and the Renault 5, perhaps the author, who also includes the Mercedes 190, can be excused on the grounds of striving too hard for effect.

Doron Levin's book on Iacocca points out that no other executive at Chrysler believed in the TC project and that when it was eventually stopped, after three years of production and a total of 7,300 cars, he refused to take the blame for its failure to meet his original targets of between five to ten thousand cars a year for

A handful of TCs have made it to the UK and this version is used as a daily driver in central London by Stephen Clahr.

Production figures

Engine	**1989**	**1990**	**1991**	**Totals**
Chrysler Turbo II	3,377	-	-	3,377
Maserati dohc	387	114	-	501
Mitsubishi V6		1,787	1,635	3,422
Totals	3,764	1901	1,635	7,300*

*In addition, one further car was built later from parts, making a grand total of 7,301.

These figures are courtesy of the TC Club. They show 1991 year models even though the production line had closed by the end of May 1990.

five years, maintaining that the car had not been marketed properly by Joe Campana, the vice-president of the Chrysler-Plymouth division.

Levin also maintains that reliability was a major factor, as the car 'literally shed parts as it rolled down the highway' – a view with which many TC owners would take issue, though fit and finish were acknowledged by some to be not of the best.

The price of the final year's cars went up sharply to $38,000; there were some small changes during the production run, in steering wheels, hardtop latches, and the woodgrain trim. Even the wiring harnesses were different, depending on who could supply them at the time.

The Maserati-engined version accounted for only 501 of the 7,300 cars built. Dr David George Briant, who has made a study of the TC, points out that this was only 6.9 per cent of the total, compared with an expected 20 per cent.

So how much of a Maserati was the TC? It was assembled in Italy by people who built real Maseratis, but there was an obvious sensitivity in Chrysler's marketing about using the name. They decreed that in publicity 'by Maserati' must be less than 80 per cent of the size of 'Chrysler TC' and the phrases 'by Maserati' or 'Built by Maserati' could not appear outside Chrysler dealerships.

Back in 1986, while the project was still being developed, a contributor to *Road & Track* wrote of Iacocca's dream of an international-style automobile:

> … you're wasting our time with that silly made-in-Italy K-car Chairman Lee. If you're serious about this you'll start selling the Maserati 425, Biturbo and Cabriolet. They're the best American luxury cars on the market.

In the end, the TC was not more successful for several reasons. The Italian honeymoon had turned sour for Chrysler, who decided to abandon the project after some $250m had been spent, and after the agreed 7,300 had been built, the line was closed.

Giving the game away

The TC had also missed its window of opportunity – a car announced in 1985 to some excitement did not turn up until 1989 and by then car buyers were becoming more sophisticated. Chrysler had thought that the car industry's long-running smoke and mirrors tricks could persuade them that they were getting a hand-built Maserati for $33,000 – but the canny consumer realized that a car very similar to a LeBaron was not worth $13,000 more because it had an Italian provenance.

The game was further given away in the interior; anyone familiar with the Chrysler range would recognize immediately the TC's steering column, foot-operated parking brake, door handles, climate controls, dashboard vents, window switches, glove box and ashtray.

There was also a confusion of identity: the TC was a rather fast, front-wheel-drive cruiser, not the type of hard-driven car associated with the Maserati name. And it had only four cylinders. One British car executive trying to sell small saloons in the USA once remarked that the average American would rather live in a four-roomed house and have an eight-cylinder car than vice versa. Had the TC been rear-wheel drive and had the Shamal's new twin overhead cam 3.2-litre V8 turbo (*see* Chapter 13), which put out 325bhp, the story might well have been different. Then there was the issue of whether it really was an Italian car or not.

It also has to be said that American/Italian automotive co-operation has never gone well since the days when Nash asked Pinin Farina, as it was called then, to design a car for its fiftieth anniversary. It was not successful, neither was the Allanté (21,000 built) or the Dodge Dual Ghia …

Nevertheless, the TC is a fine car, which has a loyal and enthusiastic following in the USA and the owners' club, TC America Inc., has an excellent website:
www.chryslertcbymaseraticlub.com.

There are at least two TCs in the UK, though neither has the Maserati engine.

7 Major improvements – the 430 and 4.24v

Porsches are for people who are going places; Maserati are for people who have arrived.

Nick May, MD Maserati (UK) Ltd, 1988

In 1987, major changes, which had been two years in gestation, were announced to update the Biturbo mechanically. They came, as by De Tomaso tradition, on 14 December that year and were introduced first on the new 430, which was seen first in the UK at the Birmingham motor show the following year.

This car was a cosmetically improved version of the 420i and 425i but had the 2.8-litre engine, which gave it 250bhp at 5,600rpm and a top speed of 150mph (240km/h). Maserati claimed a 0–62mph (100km/h) time of 5.2sec. For countries that insisted on a catalyst, there was a detuned 225bhp version. There were air-to-air intercoolers, larger turbos and the Weber Marelli injection/ignition setup.

The 430 was the fast, luxurious flagship of the Biturbo range – not that it was ever called

The name Biturbo had been dropped by the time the 430 appeared in 1988. It had softer body lines than the 425, and wheels across the range were now secured by five bolts rather than four. (Dave Smith)

a Biturbo in its publicity, as the name was to disappear in 1988 – and considerably more expensive than the other four-door saloons, retailing in Italy at the equivalent of £29,000 in February 1988, while its 2.5 sibling was some £9,000 cheaper.

De Tomaso's view was that he wanted a fast, luxurious, understated car; what Maserati produced was a modern-day classic for the most demanding buyer in the sports or luxury driving market, according to the publicity. Aurelio Bertocchi referred to it as a small Quattroporte.

It was certainly lavish: automatic climate control, electric windows and mirrors, remote power releases for boot and petrol flap, halogen headlights, rear window blinds, power-operated driver's seat, briarwood facings on the doors and console with matching gearknob and handbrake lever. Two kinds of hand-stitched leather upholstery could be specified: classic, with armchair-like front seats; and sporting, with flatter cushions and side bolsters. There was great attention to detail – the trident emblem on the rear roof pillars were inset flush with the body to reduce wind noise.

It was also said to be the first production car in the world with new and highly efficient German acoustic damping, which had primary sound-deadening and secondary vibration barriers designed to eliminate resonance in the body shell. The deep carpeting had thermal insulation.

The only options were metallic paint and an electric tilt and slide sunroof, but – at least in the version sold in Britain – there were curious omissions: still no ABS or radio/cassette player.

Softer lines

The exterior differed little from the 425. There were softer body lines, and at the front the grille was mesh and the surround more heavily chromed and less angular. The top face of the front bumper, rather than being body coloured, had stick-on stainless steel facings, though the brochure maintained that they were chrome. There were solid alloy wheels – now secured with five bolts rather than four – with 15in rims and 205/55VR tyres.

It is common among Maserati cognoscenti to distinguish the earlier Biturbos from the later models by referring to them as four-bolt or five-bolt cars. Essentially, the 430 and the rest of the range from July 1987 onwards had not only five-bolt wheels, but also a more rounded profile.

The 430 was also tested far more than earlier Biturbos before being put into production. Maserati claimed that there had been hundreds of thousands of miles of testing in punishing conditions and climates and claimed that over two years' design effort had gone into the development of the engine and chassis.

Comparing it with the 425, which, it said, displayed snappish oversteer at the limits of cornering, *Road and Track* reported that 'the new car will still hang the tail out in fast transitions, but in a more gradual and controllable fashion … delightful to drive fast but gets to be a bit of a handful if you try to push it too hard.'

Brakes were uprated, being larger, with floating calipers and self-venting discs for more bite.

Car magazine reported at the time that the chassis changes were subtle but their effect was dramatic, giving the car a more direct feel, losing the roll, pitch and dive of earlier models. 'Both on wet, twisty roads and fast motorways, the 430 is by far the best of the Biturbo series so far.'

A new limited slip differential was launched with the 430. It was said to have been designed specially by Maserati, but was in fact an off-the-shelf 3.31:1 unit from Quaife Engineering Ltd in England. Just as De Tomaso had invented the name Sensitork® for the previous Torsen differential, he now called this the Ranger®, sticking the little registered symbol after the name to imply exclusiveness.

Quaife company legend says that when Maserati tried a ZF limited slip unit, they experienced a 27 per cent failure rate, which is why they went to Quaife, though this statistic is more likely to relate to the Sensitork, which was notorious for its fragility.

Peter Knivett, Quaife's marketing manager, says that commercial reasons dictated why the Automatic Torque Biasing differential, as it is officially known, was never credited to Quaife, but he says the run of units was successful and the reliability of the units was exemplary. The unit is still in production and has been fitted to 4,500 Ford Focus RS models with no warranty claims.

The Ranger consists of a series of central gears surrounded by six satellite helical gears positioned in a star pattern. The basic advantage of this system is that all the gears work on a common axle and the output is more reliable than the traditional, plate-style limited slip differential, which uses a pack of clutch plates worked by sun and planetary gears to transmit a set percentage of the torque to the spinning wheel.

Later cars used different ratios: 3.36:1 for the manual version and 3.77:1 for the automatic gearbox. For some reason the ZF four-speed

430 Four-door saloon (1987–94)

Engine	
Type:	AM473
Layout:	V6 90 degrees – 3 valves per cylinder, single overhead cam per bank, two IHI turbochargers
Type:	AM477
	V6 90 degrees – 4 valves per cylinder, double overhead cam per bank
Bore × stroke:	94 × 67mm
Capacity:	2790cc
Compression ratio:	7.8:1
Max power:	3v 250bhp/183kW@5,600rpm 4v 279bhp@5,600rpm
Max torque:	3v 283.5lb ft/39.2kg m @3,600rpm 4v 317lb ft/43.9kg m @3,500rpm
Fuel system:	Weber Marelli injection
Intercoolers:	Two air-to-air
Transmission	
Gearbox:	ZF manual 5 speed + reverse
Final drive:	Ranger 3.31:1
Suspension	
Front:	MacPherson strut with anti-roll bar, coil springs, shock absorbers
Rear:	Trailing arms, coil springs, shock absorbers, anti-roll bar
Steering:	Power-assisted rack and pinion
Brakes:	Servo-assisted twin circuit, front and rear ventilated discs with floating calipers, rear drum parking brake
Running gear	
Wheels:	3v 6½J × 15 4v 7J × 16
Tyres:	3v 205/50VR15 (front), 225VR15 (rear) 4v 205/45 R16 (front), 225/45 ZR16 (rear)
Performance	
Max speed:	3v 149mph (240km/h) 4v 158mph (255km/h)
Acceleration:	0–62mph (100km/h) in 5.7sec
Dimensions	
Wheelbase:	94.5in (2,400mm)
Front track:	56.8in (1,442mm)
Rear track:	57.2in (1,453mm)
Length:	173.2in (4,400mm)
Width:	68.1in (1,730mm)
Height:	51.6in (1,310mm)
Weight:	2,600lb (1,180kg)
Number built	1,286

automatic cost a whopping £1,177 extra, while on the 425 it cost only £595 more.

A discrepancy between auto box costs in different engine sizes appeared across the range, and the only explanation was that the makers could get away with charging more in the larger engine sizes. Car manufacturers have traditionally charged more for a car with a few hundred more cubic centimetres, despite the fact that their production costs are much the same. The 430 cost nearly £8,000 more than the 425; was it worth paying an extra 25 per cent – even taking the 430's enhancements into consideration?

However, in the Biturbo's day car manufacturers had not yet cottoned on to the 21st-century wheeze of selling two-door coupés for more than their four-door equivalents – a classic case of paying more for less.

Blistering performance

The 430 offered blistering performance in an understated saloon – 0–100mph in 16.8sec, according to *Motor*, but at a considerable price. In July 1990, the 430 was selling in Italy for about £32,000, in the UK it was nearly £37,000, which was about £10,000 more than

The later 430s had a new black grille and integral driving lamps in the spoiler. The car was available with either the three- or four-valve engine. There was a power difference of some 50bhp between them. (Fonte Archivio Maserati)

a BMW M3 and about the same price as a BMW 63Csl. Those less well-endowed could get a Ford Sierra Cosworth 4×4 for £25,000. However, *Motor* reported that it was more than a match for the much less refined Cosworth:

> The 430 would have no problem in disposing with the Mercedes 300E, BMW 535i or Audi 200 Turbo, which, with the same level of equipment would cost roughly the same. It remains to be seen whether the Maserati's reliability and durability will match the Germans.

The 430 continued in successful low-volume production until 1991, when an even faster version, with the four-valves-per-cylinder engine, was introduced. It was first seen at the 1988 Turin motor show, though the three-valve version continued in production. This was the one that made its debut in the UK at the Birmingham motor show in October 1988. (Details of the four-valve engine are in Chapter 10.)

In the 430, the 4v variant featured a big increase in power from 225bhp to 278bhp at

Six cars in Maserati's 'New Cars for the Nineties' programme, which led to considerable improvements in suspension and mechanical reliability. However, the range was not as simple as it seems, as many variations on these models were to come. (Fonte Archivio Maserati)

La linea

Nuovi dettagli estetici: la mascherina è verniciata in nero opaco, così come le cornici dei vetri ed i due tridenti posti sui montanti posteriori.
Nuove soluzioni areodinamiche: spoiler anteriore più avvolgente; nuovi fari fendinebbia incassati a filo di spoiler che aggiungono importanza al frontale. Sul cofano due sfoghi aria per il vano motore, realizzati con due prese NACA invertite.

Vista di fianco la vettura appare più attaccata a terra grazie alla minigonna opportunamente disegnata per migliorare l'aerodinamica.
Nuovi i cerchi in lega leggera a disegno stellare con sette razze: le colonnette di fissaggio sono nascoste da un coprimozzo a forma di dado esagonale sulla cui superfice è impresso il tridente. Raffinatezza e sportività espresse anche nei minimi dettagli.

A 4.24v, sinister-looking in black, and without a hint of chrome in the grille other than the trident, was a four-door version of the Italian market 2.24v, using the 2-litre engine. (Fonte Archivio Maserati)

5,500rpm. Official top speed was now 158mph (255km/h) and the 0–62mph (0–100km/h) was unaccountably slightly slower at 6sec rather than 5.7sec.

Body changes included new front lights, which were also seen on the Shamal: two square and two low-beam polyelliptical lamps to produce very strong beams for enhanced visibility. Other body changes, seen first on the SE and carried across the rest of the range, included the new black grille with integral fog and driving lamps below the front bumper, and a similar grille at the rear through which the twin exhausts exited either side

There was also the 4.24v – a four-door version of the 2.24v. About 400 were built. Total 430 production, which ran from 1987 to 1994, was 1,286.

8 The 228

The Biturbo range had begun in 1983 with a single model; by the beginning of 1988 there were no fewer than eleven variants being offered on the Italian home market: eight 2-litre taxbreaker versions, the 425 saloon and a new large coupé – the 228.

The word Biturbo disappeared from the catalogues in the spring of 1988 as Maserati was beginning what it called a programme of 'new cars for the nineties'.

The 228 was quite simply a two-door car with a 2.8-litre engine (actually 2789cc), but it

Maserati made the 228 a larger version of the Biturbo in the hope of competing with the large German coupés of BMW and Mercedes. The 2789cc engine put out 250bhp. (Fonte Archivio Maserati)

Size comparison – 228i, 420 and 2.24v

	228i	420	2.24v
Length	14ft 7in (4,460mm)	14ft 5in (4,400mm)	13ft 9in (4,190mm)
Width	6ft 1in (1,865mm)	5ft 8in (1,730mm)	5ft 7in (1,714mm)
Height	4ft 4in (1,330mm)	4ft 5in (1,360mm)	4ft 3in (1,305mm)
Weight	2,932lb (1,330kg)	2,810lb (1,275kg)	2,751lb (1,248kg)
Wheelbase	8ft 6in (2,600mm)	8ft 6in (2,600mm)	8ft 3in (2,514mm)
Front track	5ft (1,540mm)	4ft 9in (1,442mm)	4ft 9in (1,458mm)
Rear track	5ft 1in (1,550mm)	4ft 9in (1,453mm)	4ft 9in (1,454mm)

NB *Imperial dimensions rounded to the inch*

was considerably larger than the other versions of the two-door coupé and even bigger than the 430 four-door, which was its contemporary. In fact it was the longest, widest and heaviest of the Biturbo cars and their derivatives. It was big, handsome and fast. The table (*see* above) shows how much larger the 228 was compared with the 420 and another coupé platform.

It has been suggested that the reason for building it was to replace the Quattroporte and its Royale version, which were being phased out. These were, however much bigger cars with huge engines and they had, of course, four doors and Maserati already had the 430 on offer, which Bertocchi had called his small Quattroporte.

The 228 was more likely to have been constructed to satisfy the traditional Maserati customer's desire for a GT in which lavish comfort and speed were combined, in the tradition of the 3500 of the late 1950s and early 1960s, a car that had transformed Maserati's fortunes by moving the company away from racing machines and into the serious production of road cars.

The 228 was meant to move the Biturbo range upmarket to compete with coupés like the Mercedes 300, the BMW 635 and the Bertone-designed Volvo 780, although these were all bigger and their interiors were more in tune with northern European functionalism than with Italian opulence. Despite the fact that the 228 was nearly 20mm shorter than the Mercedes, there was more room in the back.

According to the Maserati press release issued to announce the arrival of the 228 in the USA, the 228 was 'handcrafted at the legendary Milan design studio Zagato', though it does not appear in Zagato's project lists, as does the Spyder (*see* Chapter 9), and it was almost certainly designed in-house at Maserati.

The 228, first seen in the UK at a London show in 1987 and on sale from spring the following year, came at a premium price. Catalogued Maserati prices in the UK see-sawed all over the place in the 1980s and early 1990s, but in summer 1990 the 228 was heading for £50,000 and was by far the most expensive car in the Biturbo range:

June 1990

222SE	£37,450
430	£39,925
Spyder E	£41,500
Karif	£44,800
228	£48,500

It was catalogued rather cheekily as the 228 S Class coupé. Automatic transmission was another £1,295 and metallic paint £763. It is difficult to see why anyone would pay so much for the 228 when they could have a similar performing – albeit smaller – Maserati, the

228 Two-door coupé (1987–91)

Engine	
Type:	AM473
Layout:	V6 90 degrees – 3 valves per cylinder, single overhead cam per bank, two IHI turbochargers
Bore × stroke:	94 × 67mm
Capacity:	2790cc
Compression ratio:	7.7:1
Max power:	250bhp/183kW@5,600rpm
Max torque:	274lb ft/38.0kg m@3,500rpm
Fuel system:	Weber Marelli injection
Intercoolers:	Two air-to-air
Transmission	
Gearbox:	ZF manual 5 speed + reverse
Final drive:	Ranger 3.31:1
Suspension	
Front:	MacPherson strut with anti-roll bar, coil springs, shock absorbers.
Rear:	Trailing arms, coil springs, shock absorbers, anti-roll bar
Steering:	Power-assisted rack and pinion
Brakes:	Servo-assisted twin circuit, front and rear ventilated discs with floating calipers, rear drum parking brake
Running gear	
Wheels:	7J × 15
Tyres:	205/50 R15 (front) 225/50 R15 (rear)
Performance	
Max speed:	146mph (235km/h)
Acceleration:	0–62mph (100km/h) in 5.6sec
Dimensions	
Wheelbase:	102.4in (2,600mm)
Front track:	60.6in (1,540mm)
Rear track:	57.1in (1,450mm)
Length:	175.6in (4,460mm)
Width:	73.4in (1,865mm)
Height:	52.4in (1,330mm)
Weight	2,734lb (1,240kg)
Number built	469

222E, for £10,000 less. In fact the top speeds were identical at 140mph (225km/h), even though the 222E was only 2 litres. While the 228 was not initially targeted at the BMW 3 series segment of the market, it is instructive to note that at the same time a BMW M3 was even cheaper than the 222E, at £26,000.

However, there was a dramatic reduction in prices after the failure of Maserati (UK) and the taking up of the franchise by Meridien Maserati in January 1992. The new owners carried on the previous concessionaire's tradition of adding S or SE for Special Equipment to model names.

In fact, the only factory options across the range were automatic transmission on the 228S, 430SE and Spyder SE (now only £797), metallic paint and an electric sunroof on the 228S and 430SE at £950.

March 1992

222SE	£28,372
430SE	£30,082
228S	£31,730
Spyder SE	£33,240

So within two years it had become £17,000 cheaper, while the Spyder had become only £8,260 less.

In-house design

The production of the 228, which was designed in house, heralded a change of style across the range, with bodies becoming softer and rounder, losing the angularity of the earlier cars but still retaining the purposeful, wedge-shaped look.

One of the 228's selling points was the *Schalldämpffungssystem*, the Silent Travel sound suppressing system made in Germany, first seen on the 430 and subsequently installed on the rest of the range.

There were many other standard features, some not seen on some of the other cars, such as electrical seat adjustment, automatic air conditioning, electric windows and mirrors

The interior space benefited from the larger external dimensions, and the quality of the materials was improved. It had the German sound suppressing system first seen on the 430.

and, in some markets, delights such as a heated rear window with Venetian blind.

There was lavish use of burr walnut inside and the interior trim was two-tone leather, which could be had in black, blue, grey or white. The exteriors were offered in Maserati Red, Swan White, Blue Silver, Dark Aquamarine, Black and two shades of grey – Rifle Grey and Soft Grey.

The car had been first announced in 1984 at the traditional December press conference with the exciting prospect of a new engine: a V6 of 2790cc with 'electronically controlled Weber carburation', four valves and two spark plugs per cylinder. The concept of the twin-plug engine was not new to Maserati as it had appeared in the 1950s in the A6G and later in the 5000GT.

However, the twin plug failed to materialize at launch, as did the fuel injection and the four-valve head; this did not appear until 1988, so the car eventually arrived more than a year later with the new three-valve 2.8 engine, the *tipo* AM 473. This had a bore and stroke of 94 × 67mm, compared with the 2.5's 91.6 × 63mm, and was much more powerful, putting out 245bhp at 6,000rpm. There were two new water-cooled turbos.

This engine was originally fuelled by the twin-choke Weber, but only a few of these cars were built before injection arrived with the 228i, which was in a milder state of tune and also led to a slight fall-off in performance. The compression ratio was dropped from 8.5:1 to 7.7:1 (the catalyser version was even lower, at 7.4.1) and this injected engine produced 250bhp at 5,600rpm compared with 255bhp at 6,000rpm in the original carburetted model. Top speed of the 228i was more than 146mph (235km/h).

Maserati had announced that the 228's engine would be a four-valve, twin-plug unit, but it was with the standard 2.8 that it eventually appeared.

Tyres were originally 205/60VR × 15 front and rear on light alloy discs; later export versions saw 205/55VR on the front and 225/50 on the back. In these export markets, like Germany, in which the 228 was successful, the car was offered with automatic transmission as an option, firstly three-speed, then four.

'It has beastly acceleration', said *Fast Lane* in April 1987, quoting Maserati's figures of 0–62mph (0–100km/h) of 5.8sec and a top speed of 150mph (240km/h) – as usual, a rather higher maximum than any independent road test could manage.

The cost issue was brought up by the well-known motoring writer Giancarlo Perini when he tested the 228 for *Car South Africa* in early 1988: 'While it is hardly the most rational choice in terms of value for money, it is certainly a very attractive motor car.'

Marginal turbo lag

Perini reported marginal turbo lag and power surging above 3,000rpm, but added that the high power-to-weight ratio and 'really wild torque' generated by the turbos in combination

This 228 from 1990 was one of only forty-nine built in right-hand drive. Its original price when new in the UK was £48,500, but within two years the list price of 228s had come down to under £32,000.

with the 'comfort-type' suspension called for care: 'Out of tighter bends at speed, the car shows understeer and the best way to face it is to send some more torque to the rear wheels, which sometimes requires nerve.'

European *Car* magazine reported:

> The 2.8-litre, twin turbocharged V6 propels the two-door sports sedan down the highway like nothing else in its class. Nothing even comes close. A scant 6.0sec is all it takes to reach 60mph. Maximum horsepower (225) is tapped at 5,600rpm, and peak torque (246lb/ft) at 3,500rpm, but those are simply numbers. You might as well count the brush strokes on a Michelangelo.
>
> This is a car with a decidedly aggressive disposition. And, while the suspension is, naturally, softer than what you'd find in a road-going sports car, the 228 feels fairly nimble and isn't thrown off stride in the least, tail out, rounding a big sweeper. Step on it too hard coming out of a turn on a rainy afternoon, however, and you'll find yourself looking into the back seat, eye to eye with your passengers.

The Maserati Club in the UK estimates that 469 cars were built and that of these forty-nine were right-hand-drive models produced between 1988 and 1992. Depreciation on these cars was fearsome. Brian Cunningham, who still drives his 1990 example, bought his

The 228's front grille was designed to be more aggressive than the rest of the range at the time. (Dan McCallum)

Note the non-standard strut tower brace; MIE in the USA market them at around $400 for 228s and Biturbos post-1987. They are claimed to have a noticeable effect on handling. (Dan McCallum)

The same car with a four-valve engine from a Ghibli installed. It also has a five-speed Getrag 'box, instead of the standard ZF unit, which meant using a different prop shaft. (Dan McCallum)

in Glasgow when it was two years old and had done 11,000 miles. He paid £18,700; the cost new had been £48,500. (The days of catastrophic depreciation of supercars are still with us: a Ferrari 612, just over a year old, was sold at auction by Bonham's in 2005 for £99,744 – a loss of more than £70,000 on the price when it was new.)

Manuals refer to a series one and two of the 228, though the difference between them seems to be related only to steering tweaks.

There was some variation in the US import figures for the 228. For instance, in 1989, seventy-one manuals were imported against five automatics, whereas in the following year it became one manual and fifteen automatics, presumably because the 1989 manuals had not all been shifted – bearing in mind the price of $57,000 this is perhaps not surprising. The total number imported was ninety-seven.

No Maseratis of any kind were imported into the USA in 1991, and the market was abandoned soon afterwards and not re-entered for many years.

9 The Spyder

> This is a car not only for today's 'Gentleman Drivers' but for anyone who loves travelling in the open air in maximum comfort.
>
> *US Maserati brochure*

Maserati (and Porsche) have always spelled Spyder with a 'y'; Ferrari, Fiat and Alfa have preferred an 'i'. This term for a small two-seater car dated back to the early twentieth century and was said to derive from the large spider-like spoked wheels on two-seater carriages. The term really came to prominence in the early 1950s with the Porsche 550 RS Spyder, the name being revived, it is said, by the

The early Spyder range with the four-bolt wheels. (Fonte Archivio Maserati)

The first Spyders came to the UK in 1987 but would never sell in large numbers as they cost nearly £10,000 more than the BMW 325i convertible. (NMM)

The Spyder offered luxury, speed and open-top motoring at its best. It was in production for nine years – longer than any other model in the Biturbo range. (LAT)

American auto importer Johnny Von Neuman, who sold one to James Dean. The name persisted, even though there was huge publicity when Dean died in the Spyder, which disintegrated when he hit a Ford sedan driven by one Donald Turnipseed on 30 September 1955 between Hollywood and Salinas, California.

It was De Tomaso's decision to go ahead with a Spyder version of the Biturbo that revived the fortunes of Zagato, one of Italy's oldest coachbuilders. The family firm, founded in Milan after the first war, had fallen on hard times in the 1970s and the works at Terazzano di Rho, near the Alfa Romeo works at Arese, had been reduced to making armoured cars and golf carts – a far cry from the beautiful bodies that had been made for Alfas since the first Mille Miglia in 1927. They had also bodied a famous Maserati, *il monstro*, the 450S driven by Moss and Harry Schell in the 1957 Le Mans.

Zagato had begun their automotive comeback at the 1983 Geneva show, where they displayed the Alfa Zeta 6, a two-door coupé on a GTV chassis with a 3-litre engine. This was just a concept, but De Tomaso was impressed and ordered from them a Spyder version of the Biturbo. It appeared first at the Turin motor show in October 1984 and went on sale the following year.

It was not, however, the first Biturbo Spyder, as one had been on display at the Turin show two years earlier, in 1982. It was built on a very early Biturbo floorpan by the Italian *carrozzeria* Embo at Caramanga, south of Turin, who were already supplying De Tomaso with a long-wheelbase version of the Innocenti Mini and bodies for their own Pantera's later versions.

Embo had been in business since 1970, supplying one-off bodies and sheet metal pressings to the Italian car industry. Their prototype had four seats on the standard coupé wheelbase, rather than two seats on a shorter wheelbase, which was how the car eventually appeared. But Zagato, rather than Embo, went on to make the production version.

'Put a roof on it'

Though De Tomaso had personally commissioned the car from Zagato, he had been told that they did not do roofs very well, so he asked them to do just the body. It was typical of his management style that when the prototype appeared in Modena he told them to go back and put a roof on it.

There had been beautiful Maserati dropheads before; Zagato and Frua had bodied A6G chassis with convertible coachwork in the early 1950s, and the Fruas were known as Spyders. The name appeared again on a Maserati with the 3500 Spyder in 1959; that was followed in 1964 by the Mistral Spyder, designed by Frua and built by Maggiora, and in the early 1970s came what has been described many times as 'the most beautiful sports car ever built' – Giugiaro's Ghibli Spyder.

The Biturbo Spyder was based on the standard coupé, and much of the metalwork at the front was the same up to the A post. The quarter-light, which did not hinge, did not appear on the coupé, but the door skins were common.

The chassis and wheelbase were shortened and Zagato fashioned a different rear end to allow for the stowage of the folding hood – the same type that they used for the Aston Martin Volante, which was built alongside it.

The Spyder's body shell was partially pressed and assembled by a company run by Alessandro Festa, which from 1986 was called Golden Car and based at Caramanga. The rear portions were unique to the Spyder, though much of the front came from the Innocenti works at Lambrate.

The shells were then sent on to Zagato's own small workshops in Milan for further sheetmetal work, then trimming and painting. Most of this work was done by hand. At some stage, production was moved from Zagato to Maserati in Modena, possibly because of Zagato's increasing order book.

The Spyder was essentially a luxurious two-seater, in which one could indulge oneself in the *inclino orizontale* position; behind the seats was a vestigial carpeted area with two loose

Although the rear compartment had cushions, it would be impossible to sit on them facing to the front as there was no room for knees. (LAT)

cushions, into which no-one could squeeze, but which could be used for luggage.

Shorter than the coupé

The re-engineering of the rear end meant that although it was shorter than the coupé, by 4.3in (10.9cm) and had a shorter wheelbase of 94.8in (240cm) rather than 98.97in (251.4cm), the luggage capacity could be increased by 5cu ft (0.14cu m) to 19cu ft (0.54cu m).

The metal was spray-painted and then the lavish leather interior installed. As the English brochure for the Spyder iE put it:

> The interior is a trat (sic) to your eyes, hands and back. Elegant woods have been chosen for the facings on doors, dashboard and console as well as for the handles of the handbrake and gearshift.

The canvas convertible top with Alcantara headlining was added. It was attached to the top of the screen with two handles and folded back neatly into a tray at the rear. Although the rear window was Perspex, two glass rear quarter-lights folded back with the hood, which was then covered with a leather apron fixed by two press studs and locating posts. Unlike other Biturbos, the rear window was not heated. The US brochure said:

> [The Spyder] captures the magic of those first open tourers but combines modern technology to ensure total comfort in even the most appalling weather conditions.

Spyder owners were expected to be smokers: not only was there the ashtray and lighter near the handbrake, in a few versions there was also a roll-top cigarette box, taken from the De Tomaso Pantera.

A discreet Zagato badge was put on the flanks at the front. This did not appear in later brochures and the word Spyder did not appear

Spyder iE, *el placer de conducir al aire libre.*
Rodar en un Maserati Spyder iE y sentir la emoción del viento, el deseo renovado de acercarse al mundo que nos rodea con toda la exaltación de la velocidad.

Zagato pulled off a difficult trick with the Spyder as many convertibles do not look as good with the hood up as they do when it's down. (Fonte Archivio Maserati)

on the coachwork at all; it was used only in brochures.

Before all production was moved to the Maserati works at Modena, the early versions were brought from Milan, for the mechanical bits to be added. Production rates at first were set at about twenty-five a week.

As with the other models in the Biturbo family, there was a 2.0-litre version for the Italian market, and larger 2.5-litre and 2.8-litre versions for export. When the four-valve engine was introduced, it was put in only in the 2.0-litre version, as the chassis lacked the torsional stiffness to deal with the increase in power in the larger engines.

A Spyder's tale

John Duggleby had been driving a Ferrari 308 when he decided it was a rather selfish car and decided to go for something less alarming.

(John Duggleby)

I asked Bill McGrath in 1997 to find me a Biturbo and they came up with this 1989 Spyder E that had done only 10,000 miles; the owner was slightly surprised that I didn't want to see it. They sorted it out for me with things like a reconditioned radiator and new half shaft seals.

I've since done about 20,000 miles in it. It's a very nice little car but it has certain limitations: – the normal scuttle shake and the engine does not have the same sort of high speed torque as the larger cars – but it's very effective in acceleration, particularly in third gear.

We were in France once and coming round a corner we hit a brick in the middle of the road; it hit the exhaust and we carried on but later found an oil leak as it had cracked the crankcase.

It meant a new engine, but it was all covered by insurance.

Maseratis are under-rated pieces of machinery, but a lot of people have been disappointed by them because they are not cheap to maintain. You can't run a Maserati on the cheap.

Colour-coded alloys gave the early Spyders a rakish appearance. The spare wheel carrier was prominent on the first Biturbo but later became concealed as valances became deeper. (Fonte Archivio Maserati)

First US versions

The first US versions in 1986 were available with automatic transmission only and a blue convertible top. For 1987, fuel injection was added.

Because the Spyder was in production for longer than any other Biturbo model – from 1985 to 1994, outliving its stablemates – it went though the whole gamut of engine development, from the basic 2.0-litre carburettor version of the early days, though fuel injection in 1987 to the 24-valve engine shortly afterwards and catalysers for some markets in 1990. There were at least seven different engines fitted over its lifespan. The 2.0-litre was available in Spain and Italy, for instance, with or without a catalyser, which knocked 3bhp off the standard 180bhp Biturbo engine. As to the 2.5-litre engine, it had for some reason 4bhp less than the 425 saloon, putting out 192bhp at 5,500rpm and 220lb ft of torque at 3,000rpm.

Wheel rim sizes varied. The carburetted cars had 14in as standard with a 15in option. The 2.8 version had 15in wheels as standard until the last version, with 16in rims.

When *Autocar* tested the Spyder over 635 miles in 1987, including a spell in ideal conditions on the high-speed track at Millbrook, they found, as many testers had done before with the Biturbo, that their figures were well below Maserati claims of 135mph (217km/h) and 0–62mph (100km/h) in 6.5sec. The real maximum was 128mph (206km/h) and the 0–60mph (96.5km/h) time was 7.2sec, even with only one gearchange.

This 1988 2.5 Spyder has the over-elaborate wheels that tend to detract from the car's simplicity of line. (Mike Roberts)

The top would have to come up pretty quickly in the rain to avoid damage to the luxurious seating leather and Alcantara on the Spyder.

The engine was found to be at its best between 2,500–4,000rpm, running out of steam at 5,000rpm, but there was a high price to pay for using the performance – overall fuel consumption of 16.9mpg (16.7ltr/100km).

The Spyder UK imports at this stage – spring 1987 – still had the single Weber carburettor with manual choke, and the usual problems of hot starting soon manifested themselves. As to handling, the magazine found that the Spyder could be a bit of a handful at times: when putting the power on out of a corner a build-up of understeer could snap into oversteer and a spin.

While luxuriously appointed with lots of leather and wood, at £29,000 one might at least have expected a radio and central locking as well. So while it was a beautifully made car, with lots of torque, it was very expensive. Its nearest rival, the BMW 325i convertible, was a whole £9,500 cheaper. At this price the Spyder would only ever occupy a tiny part in a niche market, which was already small.

Like most of the Biturbo story, the Spyder range is complicated, but essentially the carburetted Spyders in 2.0-litre home market versions and 2.5-litre export versions were replaced in 1987 with the injected Spyder i versions, which gave a large increase in power, from 192bhp to 223bhp.

Then, from 1988 to 1994 there was the 2.8-engined car, known as the Spyder E with 245bhp in non-cat form, available with four-speed automatic or five-speed manual transmission. Also included in the range from 1991 was a four-valve version of the 2.0-litre engine, which developed 241bhp.

In 1990–91, the Spyder became designated as the iE, but before that the body had been restyled to lose some of its angularity, which had been making the car look dated. The front end was softened, and two square headlamps either side of a much narrower grille were replaced with one square and one round lamp.

The front valance, which was body-coloured, was adapted in the last Spyders to include two driving lamps. It also received the 24-valve V6 engine, with 241bhp.

This automatic version was originally bought by a Saudi Arabian princeling for one of his female relatives. As women are officially not allowed to drive in Saudi Arabia, she drove it around a specially constructed circular track in secret. It is now in the UK.

Final versions used the 'polyellipsoidal' front beams from the Shamal. (Fonte Archivio Maserati)

Seven-spoke alloys

The wheels were seven-spoke alloys like on the Shamal. At the rear there was a slatted valance and either side of it twin exhaust pipes came from rectangular slots in the bodywork.

Autocar revisited the Spyder in the summer of 1988, taking it on a continental jaunt: 'Cynical journalists had laughed "You won't get as far as Dover", but the Biturbo did us proud.'

There was solid power from the engine, the doors were well-built with solid shut-lines, and while the quality of some of the materials was superb – the cockpit was sumptuous, just the right side of boudoir ostentation in fawn Alcantara and tan leather – some of the fittings were nasty, particularly the headlamp surrounds, which had a kit car feel. They also did not like the 'useless' uncalibrated boost gauge, and made the point that many owners had muttered about: it was about time that Maserati discovered ABS.

The testers were not, however, enamoured of the odd handling. 'Intimidating unpredictability in the front end' they said, and they could not power the back wheels out of line to balance the car's handling. However, on balance it was a success: 'It covers the ground effortlessly and has such character that you can forgive its shortcomings'.

Of all Biturbos built, the Spyder was the most popular and sold more than 3,000 in a nine-year production run, though curiously it did not sell all that well in America – Spyders accounted for only 16 per cent of the total number of Biturbos imported into the USA.

At the 1993 Turin motor show, OPAC, a coachbuilding firm, based in nearby Rivalta, put forward a very good-looking prototype of a new Spyder, using the Shamal V8 engine and an electric soft-top hood. It appeared again the following year with a removable steel hard top, which was planned to be built eventually in aluminium, of which the boot and bonnet were already constructed. Its other distinguishing feature was a Ferrari-like front end, with retractable headlights. It was notionally a 2+2, but the one-piece back seats could be removed and a steel tonneau cover put in their place to make a two-seater sports car.

It is a pity that this version was not put into production, as it would have given the decade-old Spyder a new lease of life. At least two were built, and one survives in the Netherlands, owned by J. P. Van der Weele.

Better looking than the original or too Japanese in appearance? The OPAC Spyder was a brave attempt in 1993 to update a Maserati classic. (Job Genders)

The OPAC Spyder's hood tucks away neatly beneath a metal cover. (Job Genders)

The V8 Spyder, which replaced the open cars of the Biturbo era, on the ramp at Maserati's factory showroom in Modena in 2004.

Spyder (1985–94)

Injection engines for 2500i, 2.0iE, 2.8iE and 2.0 4v

Basic data:	2500i	2.0iE	2.8E	2.8iE	2.04v
Max power:	192bhp (143kW) @5,500rpm	220bhp (164kW) @6,250rpm	245bhp (182kW) @5,600rpm	225bhp (165kW) @5,500rpm	241bhp (179kW) @6,500rpm
Max torque:	236lb ft @3,000rpm	193lb ft @5,500rpm	282lb ft @3,500rpm	267lb ft @3,500rpm	318lb ft @3,750rpm

Carburettor engine – 2.0-litre from 1985

Type	AM452/09
Layout	V6 90 degrees – 3 valves per cylinder, single overhead cam per bank, two IHI turbochargers
Bore × stroke:	82 × 63.5mm
Capacity:	1996cc
Compression ratio:	7.8:1
Max power:	180bhp/134.2kW@6,000rpm
Max torque:	186.6lb ft/25.8kg m@4,400rpm
Fuel system:	Weber twin-choke carburettor
Intercoolers:	None

Carburettor engine – 2500 from 1986

Type	AM453
Layout	V6 90 degrees – 3 valves per cylinder, single overhead cam per bank, two IHI turbochargers
Bore × stroke:	91.6 × 63.5mm
Capacity:	2491cc
Compression ratio:	8.5:1
Max power:	192bhp/143.2kW@5,500rpm
Max torque:	220lb ft/30.5kg m@3,000rpm
Fuel system:	Weber twin-choke carburettor
Intercoolers:	None

Transmission

Gearbox:	ZF manual 5 speed + reverse Automatic 3-speed option
Final drive:	Sensitork 3.73:1; 2500 3.31:1; iE 2.0/2.8 Ranger

Suspension

Front:	MacPherson strut with anti-roll bar, coil springs, shock absorbers
Rear:	Trailing arms, coil springs, shock absorbers, anti-roll bar
Steering:	Power-assisted rack and pinion
Brakes:	Servo-assisted twin circuit, front and rear ventilated discs with floating calipers, rear drum parking brake

Running gear

Wheels:	6J × 14 or 7J × 15 (2.0i + 2.5); 7J × 16 (front), 8J × 16 (rear) (2.8i)
Tyres:	195/60VR 14 MXV (Spyder); 205/50 R15 (2.0i); 205/45 ZR16 (front), 225/45 ZR16 (rear) (2.8i)

Performance

Max speeds:	Between 133mph (215km/h) and 140mph (225km/h)

Number built 3,076

Dimensions

	Spyder (2.0, 2.5)	*Spyder iE (2.0)*	*Spyder 2.8iE*
Wheelbase:	94.5in (2,400mm)		
Front track:	55.9in (1,420mm)	57.2in (1,454mm)	57.4in (1,458mm)
Rear track:	56.3in (1,431mm)	57.4in (1,458mm)	57.5in (1,460mm)
Length:	159.2in (4,043mm)		
Width:	67.5in (1,714mm)		
Height:	51.4in (1,305mm)	51.6in (1,310mm)	
Weight:	2,395lb (1,086kg)	2,758lb (1,251kg)	2,966lb (1,345kg)

10 The 222, its descendants and the four-valve engine

First there was the 222 (a four-bolt car with the early suspension) then the 222E, the 2.24v, the 222SE, the Racing, the 222SR and finally the 222.4v.

Confused? You might well be. No-one could ever accuse Maserati of clarity when it came to naming its range during the late 1980s and early 1990s. It was with the introduction of the 222 in 1988 that the name Biturbo was officially consigned to history, though it lingered as a generic name for many more years, since even with the new cars little had changed since its introduction in 1982, except for underneath, where there had been major changes for the better.

On the outside, this basic body shape was beginning to look old-fashioned: rather than flush glass, the windows were still sealed with strips of stainless steel. There was hardly any change to the grille and the mounting of the four rectangular headlamps – condemned by *Motor Sport* as acting like nose-mounted aerodynamic brakes. There was no money – and would not be well into the 1990s – to retool for a new, modern body shape.

Even so, Maserati launched its 'New Cars for the 90s' programme in 1988 with the range of half a dozen models, all looking much the same since their first appearance. The major improvements were mechanical rather than cosmetic: better suspension and engine reliability.

The confusing 222 range started off fairly simply with the 222 itself, which was essentially a reworking of the basic coupé but with softer lines and a redesigned grille with a denser mesh and without the NACA ducts on the bonnet. It was a 2+2 with two doors (or two camshafts) and the familiar 2.0-litre V6 for the domestic Italian market putting out 220bhp at 6,250rpm. So far so good, and easy enough to remember.

But when the 2.8 V6 engine was installed for export markets, it could not be called the 228 as this enlarged coupé already existed, so it became known – confusingly – as the 222E.

The 222 range

	Capacity (cc)	bhp	Introduced	Production
222	1996	223@5,500rpm	1988	1,156
222E*	2790	225@5,500rpm	1988	722
2.24v	1996	245@6,200rpm	1987	1,147
222SE	2790	225@5,500rpm	1990	777
Racing	1996	283@6,250rpm	1991	230
222SR*	2790	225@5,500rpm	1991	210
222.4v	2790	279@5,500rpm	1991	130

**Catalysed version; the non-cat gave 248bhp at 5,600rpm and torque of 282lb ft (38.9kg m) at 3,500rpm*

Output was up at 225bhp, only marginally more than the 222, largely due to performance being strangled by catalysers. There were then two cosmetically updated versions of this car, the SE in 1990 followed by the SR in 1991. Finally came the installation of the four-valve-per-cylinder engine, which was 2 litres in the 2.24v and 2.8 in the 222.4v.

The range was built between 1988 and some time in 1994. It is difficult to give end dates for production, as cars hung around in the factory for more than a year in some cases.

The 222E

In Britain the 222E, with its 2.8-litre engine, was the cheapest of the five-car Maserati range in the autumn of 1990, but still retailed at £37,450. It was promoted as an alternative to the Porsche 944, whose turbo version was £42,770, though the S2 was only £34,600. It is worth pointing out that in Italy at the same time, the domestic market 222 – same car with the 2.0-litre engine – retailed at the sterling equivalent of only £21,500.

In the rest of the Maserati range, the 430 was now £40,000, the Spyder SE £41,500, the Karif £44,800 and the 228SE coupé £48,500. For purposes of comparison with other Italian exotica, De Tomaso's Pantera GTS was £47,600 and the cheapest Ferrari, the Mondial, £60,500. But you could also get a Lancia Integrale for only £21,000, admittedly only in left-hand drive.

'The 222E is an anachronism', declared *Performance Car*. 'It reeks of the late 1970s, the chassis technology is barely more recent and the engine packs a wild punch no other manufacturer would dare to give a 1990s car.' The magazine went on to say that since the car was so lacking in sophisticated technology, owners were paying a high price for a high level of equipment and for the Maserati name and tradition.

This was rather unfair as a blanket condemnation: the 222E still did not have ABS, but the

222E two-door coupé* (1988–92)

Engine	
Type	AM473
Layout	V6 90 degrees – 3 valves per cylinder, single overhead cam per bank, two IHI turbochargers
Bore × stroke:	94 × 67mm
Capacity:	2790cc
Compression ratio:	7.8:1
Max power:	248bhp/182kW@5,600rpm
Max torque:	282lb ft/39.04kg m@3,500rpm
Fuel system:	Weber Marelli injection
Intercoolers:	2 air-to-air
Transmission	
Gearbox:	ZF manual 5 speed + reverse
Final drive:	Ranger 3.31:1
Suspension	
Front:	MacPherson strut with anti-roll bar, coil springs, shock absorbers
Rear:	Trailing arms, coil springs, shock absorbers, anti-roll bar
Steering:	Power-assisted rack and pinion
Brakes:	Servo-assisted twin circuit, front and rear discs with floating calipers, rear drum parking brake
Running gear	
Wheels:	7J × 15
Tyres:	205/50 R15
Performance	
Max speed:	149mph (240km/h)
Acceleration:	n/a
Dimensions	
Wheelbase:	99in (2,514mm)
Front track:	56.8in (1,442mm)
Rear track:	57.1in (1,450mm)
Length:	163.5in (4,153mm)
Width:	67.5in (1,714mm)
Height:	49.4in (1,255mm)
Weight	2,584lb (1,172kg)
Number built	722

**The 222SE was a cosmetically updated version of the 222E with deeper bumpers etc. 777 were produced 1990–94*

Maserati craftsmanship is evident in the wooden fillets and well-trimmed doors.

Bonnet ducts appeared first in the Biturbo S in 1983 and were carried through in different shapes and sizes on some, but not all, models. These are on a 222E.

Alcantara bolsters tend to wear, but the seats in this 1990 222E look almost new.

This unusual colour scheme on a 222E was ordered for a show-biz family. It is one of two cars with a 2.8-litre, 18-valve engine and improved performance package offered as an option by Maserati UK according to the present owner. Bigger turbos and other tweaks have pushed power up from 245bhp to 290bhp. (Mike Roberts)

intercooled turbo engine with its Marelli engine management and Weber sequential fuel injection system was highly sophisticated. There had also been substantial improvements to the front suspension.

However, the wayward rear end let it down yet again, according to *Performance Car*: 'It's a mystery how the Maserati testers have managed to get the front suspension and grip reasonable and the rear so wrong. They obviously like going sideways.'

Test results showed a 0–60mph (96km/h) speed of 6.6sec and a maximum of 142mph (228km/h) on the Millbrook speed bowl, 7mph down on the Maserati claim.

As with so many Biturbo tests before and after, the conclusion was that the interior was sumptuous, the engine terrific on boost, the straight-line performance a blast, but the handling indifferent to poor and not, in this case, up to the standard of its stated competitor, the Porsche 944.

One interesting problem emerged during this test, which has troubled other 222 and some other owners and was apparently well known to the Maserati dealers who fixed it: if the sump collides with anything, the engine immediately switches itself off and cannot be restarted. There is a sensor mounted on the front of the engine, underneath the front crankshaft pulley, that will switch to open circuit after a knock. While it will prevent the engine running with a cracked sump and losing oil, this a coincidence, as the primary purpose of the sensor is related to the injection system.

The 222SE

This was a cosmetically updated version of the 222E, launched in 1990. The difference

The 222 rear spoiler looked what it was – an add-on.

between an E and SE was the same on 222, 430 and Spyder. SE stood for Sports Equipment. The package with the 2.8 engine included new, deeper bumpers with integral front fog lights and the exhausts exiting within the bumper instead of underneath. Colours were typically red over grey, still with the original old-fashioned rectangular headlights.

To confuse matters further, there had already been an SE modification for the UK market available on the earlier carburettor cars, which used a Zender body kit and different wheels.

The four-valve engine

Strictly speaking this was a 24-valve engine, although Maserati always referred to it as the 4v. There was nothing new in an engine with four valves per cylinder – one had been made as long ago as 1916 by the Linthwaite-Hussey Motor Co. of Los Angeles as a way of boosting power by getting mixture in and exhaust out as quickly as possible.

A four-valve head had been built by Ernesto Maserati in 1939 for the 4CL racer – a 1½-litre straight four with a Roots blower – but Aurelio Bertocchi had insisted in the early 1980s that a four-valve configuration was not possible for the Biturbo's V6, sticking to the two intake and one exhaust per cylinder layout.

There had been some work done on a four-valve prototype in the mid-1980s, at the same time as the six-valve experiment, and now here it was, the same unit with an extra exhaust valve per cylinder, with four overhead camshafts operating the twenty-four valves.

Of the two cams on each bank of cylinders, one is belt-driven from the crank, the other driven by a chain at the rear of the engine. This has proved something of a maintenance nightmare in the 2.24 and later cars that used the same engine, right up to the last Ghiblis and V6 Quattroportes (*see* the section on buying and restoration).

This remarkable new 2.0-litre engine, which had new IHI turbos, developed 245bhp at 6,200rpm and torque of 223lb ft (30.8kg m) at 5,000rpm. Though power peaked at 5,000rpm,

The four-valve engine – strictly speaking the 24-valve – arrived first in the Italian home market 2.24v. The re-working of the head and the additional exhaust valve pushed the power of the 2.0-litre engine up to 245bhp, with most of the torque in the lower rev range.

95 per cent of the torque was available at 3,500rpm. It was the same 82 × 63mm block that had begun the Biturbo line (1996cc capacity and 180bhp), but it now had 36 per cent more power.

The 2.24v

This formidable double overhead camshaft engine was used for the first time in 1987 in the new 2.24v, produced primarily for the Italian home market and featuring active mechanical front suspension, power steering, disc brakes all round and a Ranger differential. The Koni electronically adjustable suspension was an option, costing the equivalent of £750.

The new engine pushed the car to 62mph (100km/h) in only 5.9 seconds and gave a top speed of more than 143mph (230km/h) – quart-sized performance from a pint pot. The car had the body of the 222, with the old lights but newer bumpers and the five-bolt wheels.

'The 2.24v. provides Q-car ability with performance figures that make Latin, British and Teutonic supercars flinch', declared *Motor Sport*. 'In the 0–62mph (100km/h) stakes it can hold its own with monsters like the Ferrari Testarossa, Aston Martin Virage and Porsche 928.' It could not, of course, compete with them on maximum speed.

There was also evidence that quality had improved dramatically since the early 2.0-litre cars: 'Panel fit was excellent and all other external details were of high quality while evidencing an essence of hand-built craftsmanship.'

The 2.24v was upgraded to what is often called the Phase II, with a facelift that rounded the corners and edges of the car, sideskirts, and new front and rear spoilers and alloy spoked wheels.

The Koni electronic suspension became standard and there were further changes to the rear suspension. The interior of the car was also upgraded. From 1992, all cars were fitted with a catalyser, though many Italians removed it to boost power. Just over 1,000 cars were built.

2.24v (1987–93)

Engine	
Type	AM475
Layout	V6 90 degrees – 4 valves per cylinder, double overhead cam per bank, two IHI turbochargers
Bore × stroke:	82 × 63.5mm
Capacity:	1996cc
Compression ratio:	7.6:1
Max power:	245bhp/177kW@6,200rpm
Max torque:	246lb ft/34kg m@3,000rpm
Fuel system:	Weber Marelli injection
Intercoolers:	2 air-to-air
Transmission	
Gearbox:	Getrag manual 5 speed + reverse
Final drive:	Ranger 3.77:1
Suspension	
Front:	MacPherson strut with anti-roll bar, coil springs, shock absorbers
Rear:	Tubular trailing arms, coil springs, shock absorbers, anti-roll bar; optional electronic control
Steering:	Power-assisted rack and pinion
Brakes:	Servo-assisted twin circuit, front and rear discs with floating calipers, rear drum parking brake
Running gear	
Wheels:	7J × 16
Tyres:	205/50 ZR 16
Performance	
Max speed:	140mph (230km/h)
Acceleration:	0–62mph (100km/h) in 6.1sec
Dimensions	
Wheelbase:	99in (2,514mm)
Front track:	57.2in (1,454mm)
Rear track:	57.4in (1,458mm)
Length:	164.3in (4,174mm)
Width:	67.5in (1,714mm)
Height:	51.2in (1,300mm)
Weight	2,900lb (1,300kg)
Number built	1,401

You were more likely to see the back end of this 2.24v than the front. (Matthew Leak)

The highly tuned 2.0-litre in the 2.24v produces 245bhp. The same bottom end was also used in the Ghibli, including the 330bhp Cup.

The 2.24v's leather and Alcantara interior by Ottavio Missoni is much less lurid than some of his other creations. (Derek Leak)

The 2.24v was made between 1989 and 1993 for the Italian market only and numbered just over 1,000 cars, of which fewer than 750 were this non-cat version. The car shown here is an import now registered in the UK. (Derek Leak)

The Racing

The Racing, announced in December 1990, was a high-performance version of the 2.24v coupé and regarded as the prototype for the forthcoming Ghibli. Despite its name, cast on the cam covers, it was intended for the road rather than the track. Journeys would always be pleasant, said the Italian brochure, whether they were long or in congested towns. There was no mention of competition.

The 1996cc engine was all-aluminium, rather than being light alloy with cast liners like the rest of the range. It was claimed that it had a new crankshaft, forged rather than cast pistons, lighter connecting rods, sodium-cooled valves in re-designed combustion chambers, reprofiled cams and new turbochargers, the IHI type RHM 5.2. It seems unlikely that these improvements were restricted to the Racing, but they are not mentioned in connection with the rest of the range.

The Racing's engine was said to produce 283bhp at 6,250rpm, a huge output for a 2.0-litre engine, equating to 140bhp per litre – the highest of any production road car in the world at the time – and capable in factory figures of propelling it from 0–62mph (100km/h) in 5.9sec and to a maximum of 159mph (266km/h). Of course, very large factory figures like these can be achieved by turning up the boost – at the expense of engine longevity.

There was a powerful torque curve from 2,000rpm: at 3,500rpm it was 269.8lb ft (37.3kg m) with a maximum of 275.6lb ft (38.1kg m) at 4,250rpm. Catalysts were not fitted. 'To provide a car with such readily available power, which compares to any high performance grand routier, bears witness to the sureness of the Maserati engineers in mastering the Biturbo technique', claimed the publicity.

The suspension improvements were carried over from the 2.24v: there were larger brake discs, a Getrag gearbox (more precise than the ZF box), a Ranger differential and the four-settings Koni electronic suspension.

222 two-door coupé (1988–94)

Engine

Type	AM471
Layout	V6 90 degrees – 3 valves per cylinder, single overhead cam per bank, two IHI turbo-chargers
Bore × stroke:	82 × 63.5mm
Capacity:	1996cc
Compression ratio:	7.8:1
Max power:	223bhp/166kW@6,200rpm
Max torque:	193lb ft/26.7kg m@3,500rpm
Fuel system:	Weber Marelli injection
Intercoolers:	2 air-to-air

Transmission

Gearbox:	ZF manual 5 speed + reverse
Final drive:	Torsen 3.727:1

Suspension

Front:	MacPherson strut with anti-roll bar, coil springs, shock absorbers
Rear:	Trailing arms, coil springs, shock absorbers, anti-roll bar
Steering:	Power-assisted rack and pinion
Brakes:	Servo-assisted twin circuit, front and rear discs with floating calipers, rear drum parking brake

Running gear

Wheels:	7J × 14
Tyres:	205/50 R15

Performance

Max speed:	138mph (225km/h)
Acceleration:	n/a

Dimensions

Wheelbase:	99in (2,514mm)
Front track:	56.8in (1,442mm)
Rear track:	57.1in (1,450mm)
Length:	164.3in (4,174mm)
Width:	67.5in (1,714mm)
Height:	51.2in (1,300mm)
Weight	2,670lb (1,210kg)

Number built n/a

Racing two-door coupé (1990–92)

Engine

Type	AM490
Layout	V6 90 degrees – 4 valves per cylinder, double overhead cam per bank, two IHI turbochargers
Bore × stroke:	82 × 63.5mm
Capacity:	1996cc
Compression ratio:	7.6:1
Max power:	283bhp/208kW@6,250rpm
Max torque:	275lb ft/38.1kg m@4,250rpm
Fuel system:	Weber Marelli injection
Intercoolers:	2 air-to-air

Transmission

Gearbox:	ZF manual 5 speed + reverse
Final drive:	Ranger 3.77:1

Suspension

Front:	MacPherson strut with anti-roll bar, coil springs, shock absorbers
Rear:	Trailing arms, coil springs, shock absorbers, anti-roll bar; electronic suspension optional
Steering:	Power-assisted rack and pinion
Brakes:	Servo-assisted twin circuit, front and rear ventilated discs with floating calipers, rear drum parking brake

Running gear

Wheels:	7J × 16
Tyres:	205/45 ZR 16 (front) 225/45 ZR 16 (rear)

Performance

Max speed:	159mph (256km/h)
Acceleration:	0–62mph (100km/h) in 5.9sec

Dimensions

Wheelbase:	99in (2,514mm)
Front track:	57.4in (1,458mm)
Rear track:	57.2 (1,454mm)
Length:	165.2in (4,195mm)
Width:	67.5in (1,714mm)
Height:	51.4in (1,305mm)
Weight	2,917lb (1,323kg)

Number built 230

The Racing – available only in red and black – has sometimes been described as a prototype for the Ghibli. Despite having its name cast into the cam covers it was a road rather than a track car. The 1996cc engine was all aluminium. (Fonte Archivio Maserati)

Externally there were colour-coded mirrors and deeper side skirts. Body colours were only two, red or black, with black leather interiors. The wheels were the Shamal's 16in, seven-spoke OZ alloys, with the nuts hidden behind lockable hub caps.

The front looked much like the Shamal, *un look molto moderno* as the brochure put it, with its projector beam headlights. Inside, there was new instrumentation, with white figures on black backgrounds, a speedometer calibrated to 300km/h, despite a maximum of 240km/h, and an external temperature gauge.

The 222SR

The SR was first seen at the Geneva motor show in 1991. It was an updated version of the 2.8-litre 222SE using the front-end look of the Shamal, with its menacing front end and distinctive headlamp array of two square and two round lights, though with less pronounced NACA ducts. As the brochure put it, 'The front end has an ultra-modern look; the grille is slimmer and more rounded but still retains the family feeling of the current range.'

There was a spoiler underneath the windscreen like on the Shamal, and another on the boot. The Koni electronic suspension was an optional extra, as was a four-speed automatic gearbox, a heavy item that added 53lb (24kg) to the weight compared with a manual car.

The 222 4v

This was essentially the same car as the 222SR, and went into production at the same time, but with the four-valve engine. The Koni suspension was standard and it came only with the five-speed Getrag manual gearbox. It gave 278bhp rather than the SR's 225bhp, and considerably more torque: 317.5lb ft (43.9kg m) at 3,750rpm rather than 267.6lb ft (37kg m) at 3,500rpm.

Apart from the usual luxurious wood and leather specification common to both, such as climate control, tinted glass and rear window blinds, the 4v had an outside temperature thermometer. This is the rarest of the 222 series.

222SR and 222 4v two-door coupé (1991–94)

Engine	*222SR*	*222 4v*
Type	AM473	AM 477
Layout	V6 90 degrees – 3 valves per cylinder, single overhead cam per bank, two IHI turbochargers	V6 90 degrees – 4 valves per cylinder, double overhead cam per bank
Bore × stroke:	94 × 67mm	
Capacity:	2790cc	
Compression ratio:	7.4:1	
Max power:	225bhp/165kW@ 5,500rpm	278bhp/205kW@ 5,500rpm
Max torque:	267lb ft/37kg m@3,500rpm	317lb ft/43.9kg m@3,750rpm
Fuel system:	Weber Marelli injection	
Intercoolers:	2 air-to-air	
Transmission		
Gearbox:	ZF manual 5 speed + reverse; 4 speed auto	
Final drive:	Ranger 3.31:1 (manual) 3.73:1 (auto)	Ranger 3.36:1
Suspension		
Front:	MacPherson strut with anti-roll bar, coil springs, shock absorbers	
Rear:	Trailing arms, coil springs, shock absorbers, anti-roll bar Electronic suspension standard on 4v, optional on 222SR	
Steering:	Power-assisted rack and pinion	
Brakes:	Servo-assisted twin circuit. Front and rear discs with floating calipers. Rear drum parking brake	
Running gear		
Wheels:	7J × 15	7J × 16
Tyres:	205/50 R15	205/45 ZR 16 (front) 225/45 ZR 16 (rear)
Performance		
Max speed:	136mph (220km/h)	158mph (255km/h)
Acceleration:	0–62mph (100km/h) 6.2sec	6.0sec
Dimensions		
Wheelbase:	99in (2,514mm)	
Front track:	57.4in (1,458mm)	57.1in (1,450mm)
Rear track:	57.5in (1,460mm)	57.6in (1,462mm)
Length:	163.5in (4,153mm)	
Width:	67.5in (1,714mm)	
Height:	51.4in (1,305mm)	51.2in (1,300mm)
Weight	2,884lb (1,308kg) (man)	2,900lb (1,315kg)
Number built	210	130

The 222 4v introduced not only the more powerful engine, but also changes to the rear suspension.

11 The Karif and its throbbing horses

From the moment it was created there was never any doubt that the Karif would become a collector's item.

Maserati brochure

The Karif was the first of the Biturbo line to revert to the Maserati convention of naming cars after winds, in this case a monsoon wind in Somalia. It was meant to be even more overtly 'rorty' than the rest of the range – a high-speed sports car rather than a fast grand tourer – and claimed to be the fastest Maserati since the Bora of the 1970s.

It was built on the floorpan of the Spyder and, according to Maserati insiders, was the idea of a close and dear friend of De Tomaso's known as Mrs Valdevit, who persuaded him to build a hardtop version of the convertible. But

The Karif, built on the Spyder's platform, was the same size as a Ford Escort, but had the performance of a Ferrari 328GTB. It was said to be Maserati's fastest car since the Bora. (LAT)

KARIF

The Karif was launched in May 1988, and cost a staggering £44,800 in the UK in 1990. (Fonte Archivio Maserati)

it was very small for a supercar: the same size as a Ford Escort and only 3in (76.2mm) longer than Fiat's tiny Bertone-styled X1/9.

De Tomaso was anxious to point out that there were already supercars in the Maserati range – the 430 and the 228 – but these were not as fast as the Karif, which, he said, harked back to the 1950s and 1960s when Maserati built road cars that could also be racing cars. It would not compete with a Ferrari, he said, but would be priced close to the GTB.

The brochure talked of 'an exceptional road "animal", an exciting driving experience, an invitation to feel like a racing driver again or, for the first time, the subtle pleasure of feeling the throb of so many horses and of knowing you can control them.' It claimed that the engine was derived from motor racing, tuned to correspond to recent regulations on air and noise pollution.

Sitting behind the twin air-to-air intercoolers were alleged to be 285 throbbing horses in the V6, 2.8-engined version – 25bhp more than the standard 2.8 coupé. On paper these could propel the Karif to more than 158mph (255km/h); the catalysed model had 225bhp, and was some 15mph (24km/h) slower.

Maserati claimed a 0–62mph (0–100k/h) time of 4.8sec. So was this astounding figure true, or was it another example of Maserati over-egging the performance pudding? De

Tomaso maintained stoutly at the launch: 'The figure is not an estimate, it is the actual figure we managed.' Achieved, however, by former F1 driver Giancarlo Baghetti, then working for Maserati, in a works car. When a journalist dared to ask when the press would be able to try the Karif to verify this extraordinary figure, De Tomaso unleashed a torrent of abuse.

To put this figure into perspective, the new 2006 Jaguar XK coupé, with a 300bhp, 4.2-litre V8 engine and aluminium body, takes 6.2sec from 0–62mph.

Independent verification of all the Karif's power and performance claims is difficult to find, and there is a suspicion that the production engine was more like 245bhp rather than 285, though both figures were quoted in various brochures.

In fact, a road test by *Motor* in June 1988 did give an output figure of 250bhp at 5,700rpm and a torque rating of 248lb ft at 3,600rpm. This gave a 0–60mph time of 6.1sec and a top speed of what it described as nearer to 150mph (240km/h) than 160mph (257km/h), which suggests it was not tested at the limit.

Nevertheless, it was very powerful – its 89bhp per litre was among the highest of any production car. De Tomaso, with his usual bombast and a straight face, claimed at the launch, 'The engine is quite different from anything else that has gone before.' And for this there was a premium price to pay.

Motor was content to point out that it was the same engine as in the 430 and 228. It was, in fact, also mechanically identical to the 222E, which was far cheaper.

De Tomaso also said that an enormous amount of time had been spent developing the suspension and final drive. The waywardness of the Biturbo's early suspension at speed was addressed with a new setup called *meccanica attiva* – active suspension, a system of pivots designed to be much more stable on bends and slippery surfaces, and also allowed the fitting of larger wheels for a better steering feel.

Rear suspension was the standard semi-trailing arms mounted on a subframe with Bilstein shock absorbers. These improvements did not, however, curb the Biturbo's tail-happy behaviour in the wet significantly, though overall handling was said to be much improved and it was much more chuckable than the rest of the Biturbos.

But the short wheelbase and light weight could give interesting handling. 'Apply the power too generously when cornering on a damp bend and the tail will step sharply out and your £40,000 car may be heading for rapid depreciation', noted *Car*.

Braking was upgraded with ventilated discs and floating calipers. The handbrake worked on two drums in the centre of the rear discs.

Rather than the fragile Sensitork rear end, the Karif had the Ranger differential with a final drive ratio of 3.31:1, and Maserati claimed it had a 100 per cent lock-up capability, giving it traction comparable to a four-wheel drive. 'Obviously untrue', retorted *Car*.

On the *autostrada* to Bologna, *Motor*'s testers found it very stable at high speed with the turbo boost coming in at 1,700–1,800rpm; the engine was smooth, though the ZF 'box was notchy. Road behaviour was well sorted and there was impressive grip from the fat, 225-section Pirellis. The verdict: 'We didn't expect it to be so good.' *Car* tested it on the Pirelli track and agreed about the engine:

> For such a little car ... there is a marvellous absence of frenzy about the way that the Karif accelerates ... don't be deceived by the quiet engine note. The Karif is a supercar not far short of the Countach/Testarossa league. Ferrari GTBs are easy meat. Ditto the 944 Turbo SE.

The Karif was shown for the first time at the Geneva motor show in March 1988. This was not a good year for De Tomaso: early Maserati profits had turned to large losses, and to keep going he was forced to sell 49 per cent of the company to Fiat for the equivalent of £58m. Even so the model launches, as with the Karif, continued, with De Tomaso maintaining that he would like to have brought out a supercar like this ten years before, but lacked the money.

But the financial situation was now worse than it had been for some years and this is probably the reason why the Karif turned out to be rather a disappointment – despite the good reviews – as all the talk of being a racing driver again and *un frontale aggressivo* could not conceal the fact that this was recognizably still a Biturbo coupé (déjà vu styling, said *Car*) whose performance was not all that different to the 228, though it was of course cheaper – on the Italian market it cost the equivalent of £28,000, some £2,700 less than the 228.

It was also smaller, as it was based on the floor-pan and part of the body of the Spyder, which led many to refer to it as a hardtop version of the convertible. Like the Spyder, it was fashioned by Zagato in 2+2 form; the wheelbase was the same at 94.9in (2,400mm) as was the length of 158in (4,043mm). The reworking of the rear end allowed a larger boot than the Spyder's, and the hardtop treatment led to a much smaller rear window with thicker pillars than the other coupés.

So it was not exactly a pretty car – De Tomaso would not say who styled it, not even attributing it to the builders, Zagato – and one

Putting a hardtop on the Spyder led to the Karif having a smaller rear window and thicker pillars than the standard coupé.

Right-hand-drive manufacture

The export market for right-hand-drive cars was the UK, Australia, Malaysia, Singapore, Thailand and Hong Kong. These cars were not built for more than three years after the start of Biturbo production.

Biturbo right-hand-drive production figures 1986 to 1998

Model	Total	1986	1987	1988	1989	1990	1991	1992	1993	1994	1995	1996	1997	1998
Biturbo 2.5-litre	151	9	67	75										
Biturbo 2.5-litre injection	22		22											
Spyder 2.5-litre	98	1	67	30										
Spyder 2.5-litre injection	47		45	2										
425	117	13	77	26	1									
425i	44		44											
Spyder 2-litre	8					1		5	2					
Spyder 2.8-litre	147			1	78	53	2	9	4					
228i	49			2	35	10	1	1						
Karif	32			1	30	1								
430/2-litre	65				45	6	9	1	4					
430/2.8-litre	151			4	85	19	6	25	12					
222/ 222Si/ 222SR 2-litre	76				44	13	9	9	1					
222/ 222Si/ 222SR	0													
2.8-litre	118			3	73	18	6	18						
Shamal	23							11	5		7			
222 4v	11							10	1					
Ghibli 2-litre	44										18	1	25	
Ghibli 2.8-litre	133								9		51	30	18	25
Quattroporte 2-litre	3										2	1		
Quattroporte 2.8-litre	93										46	28	7	12
Quattroporte V8	32												23	9
		23	322	144	391	121	33	89	38	0	124	60	73	46

Thanks to Maserati and to Signor Ermanno Cozza, the Maserati Archivist.

Karif two-door two-seat coupé (1988–91)

Engine	
Type	AM473
Layout	V6 90 degrees – 3 valves per cylinder, single overhead cam per bank, two IHI turbochargers
Bore × stroke:	94 × 67mm
Capacity:	2790cc
Compression ratio:	7.8:1
Max power:	285bhp/210kW@6,000rpm
Max torque:	318lb ft/44kg m@4,000rpm
Fuel system:	Weber Marelli injection
Intercoolers:	2 air-to-air
Transmission	
Gearbox:	ZF manual 5 speed + reverse
Final drive:	Ranger 3.31:1
Suspension	
Front:	MacPherson strut with anti-roll bar, coil springs, shock absorbers
Rear:	Trailing arms, coil springs, shock absorbers, anti-roll bar
Steering:	Power-assisted rack and pinion
Brakes:	Servo-assisted twin circuit, front and rear ventilated discs with floating calipers, rear drum parking brake
Running gear	
Wheels:	7J × 15
Tyres:	205/50VR15 (front) 225VR15 (rear)
Performance	
Max speed:	158mph (255km/h)
Acceleration:	0–62mph (100km/h) in 4.8sec
Dimensions	
Wheelbase:	94.5in (2,400mm)
Front track:	57.3in (1,455mm)
Rear track:	57.5in (1,460mm)
Length:	159.2in (4,043mm)
Width:	67.5in (1,714mm)
Height:	51.6in (1,310mm)
Weight:	2,825lb (1,281kg)
Number built	221

unkind comment described it as a Biturbo with a slice cut out of the middle. This 4.5in (114.3mm) slice out of the wheelbase made the rear end look as if it had been compacted and the car lacked the elegance of the Spyder, even though it was the same size.

However, the performance and comfort more than made up for the exteriors aesthetic failings. As *Car* put it: 'Add the seating comfort to the unbridled cockpit luxury and you realise you are in a supercar that pampers as well as entertains.'

In the autumn of 1990, the Karif was £44,800 (equivalent £32,770 in Italy), which shows that the British driver was paying a high price for right-hand drive; but the volumes were so small – only 150 Maseratis had been sold in Britain the previous year – that even with big margins, the importers would still struggle.

Total production was tiny – 221 were sold, one to the somewhat obscure Swiss dramatist Friedrich Dürrenmatt. There were thirty-two right-hand-drive models. The colours available were Swan White, Dark Aquamarine, Maserati Red and Black.

12 The first Quattroportes and the V8

The four-door – a name that has served Maserati well for more than forty years and continues to do so – but was there ever a more uninspiring appellation name for such an outstanding car?

Yet it must have seemed logical at the time, after producing two-door coupés, for Maserati to call their first large saloon the Quattroporte. It sounds like a name that was used in the development stages then stuck into production – after all, that's how the Biturbo got its name.

Though this book covers the Maserati story in the 1980s and 1990s, it is worth briefly recounting the Quattroporte story before the De Tomaso era began. The Quattroporte is forever associated with the V8 engine – even though there was a V6 version at one stage.

The magnificent V8

Maserati had produced a light alloy V8 engine as early as 1935, for use in the RI racing car. It had a capacity of 4788cc with a single overhead camshaft for each cylinder bank. The castings came from the Milanese manufacturer Isotta Fraschini, with whom Maserati had done business since the early 1920s.

This unit was not particularly successful, though the car in which it was placed, the *tipo* V8R1, won the Pau Grand Prix in 1936. It was short-lived as Maserati returned to in-line fours and sixes for their racing programme, dabbling occasionally with a V12.

The origins of the docile yet potent V8 that was to power a new and sensational generation of Maserati road cars also lay in racing. Guido Taddeucci began work in 1954 on a 4477cc V8 and the design first appeared in 1956 in the *Tipo* 450S racer, putting out 400bhp at 7,200rpm. The car had mixed fortunes, winning at Sebring but failing to finish in the Mille Miglia and at Le Mans.

A revised version of the engine turned up next in 1958 in the 420M Eldorado, a single-seater sponsored by the eponymous ice cream maker. New regulations unifying American and European race standards now specified a maximum engine size of 4200cc, so capacity was reduced to 4190cc, though power was up to 410bhp at 8,000rpm. This was the car raced at Monza by Stirling Moss until he was forced out by faulty steering.

The first road use of the V8 came shortly afterwards in the extravagant 5000GT coupé, the first commissioned by the Shah of Iran. It was now just under 5 litres and the V8 appeared in various sizes of 4136cc, 4719cc and 4900cc throughout the 1960s and 1970s in cars like the first Ghibli, Mexico and Indy and Kyalami.

The first big saloon

The first Quattroporte, a luxury grand tourer built for four, was designed and initially bodied by Pietro Frua, coachbuilder to royalty. It appeared at the Turin show in November 1963. It was big and heavy, but it was also elegant and at its 143mph (230km/h) maximum, the fastest four-door car in the world – ideal for the new *autostrade* of Italy.

Road and Track called it the world's most luxurious four-door car and it was one of the last of the opulent, hand-built confections of the Italian motor industry: design, as we said by Frua, mechanics by Maserati, body constructed by Maggiora, leather by Connolly, painting and trimming by Vignale, bought by Peter Ustinov, Stewart Granger, the Aga Khan, Prince Rainier of Monaco, Leonid Breznev …

'This is one of the super status vehicles of the present day – a car so cleverly disguised that only the "right" people will recognise your importance', commented *Car and Driver*.

The Quattroporte 1 as it has now become known – to distinguish it from the four that have followed – used a four-cam V8 engine, bearing some superficial relationship to the unit that had originally appeared in the 450S, but tuned this time for torque rather than speed.

The 4136cc unit developed 260bhp at a rather lazy 5,500rpm. A bored-out version of 4.7 litres, which gave 290bhp, became available in the mid-1960s as an option. Both had twin overhead camshafts per bank of cylinders and were fed by four Weber 38 DCNL5 carburettors sitting on an inlet manifold in the centre of the 90-degree V.

Racing versions of this engine had had twin-plug ignition using magnetos, and it was modified for road use with coil ignition and single plugs, though the casting for the second plug hole existed for many years on the road cars.

Transmission to the De Dion rear axle was by ZF five-speed manual with the option of a three-speed Borg Warner automatic. This was later replaced with a more conventional axle. The 0–62mph (100km/h) time was 8sec and it could cruise at more than 125mph (200km/h).

Production ran to the start of the 1970s with about 750 being turned out; versions from late 1965 had double headlamps. It's believed that many have been broken for parts for replicas of the 450S. A few right-hand-drive versions were made; in the UK the car cost more than a Rolls-Royce.

Citroën's Quattroporte – the II

The Quattroporte II, designed by Bertone, was born in the Citroën era and first displayed at the Turin and Paris motor shows in 1974. Since Citroën wanted to maximize the use of its own components, the car used the French firm's brakes, hydro-pneumatic suspension and steering. In place of the V8 there was the 3-litre V6 engine built by Maserati for the Merak and the Citroën SM and it was, of course, front-wheel drive – and seriously underpowered.

It was an elegant car, with a smooth aerodynamic shape to reduce wind noise. Inside, apart from the usual refinements of air conditioning and leather it was notable for having retractable sun blinds on all the side windows.

The oil crisis of the mid-1970s and the collapse of Citroën put paid to it after only a handful were built, and it was never homologated. A few examples hung around the factory for several years until they were broken up. Some reports say that up to twenty-two were built – others just a handful.

This brings us into the De Tomaso era; he hated the complications of Citroën designs and was unwilling to resurrect their version of the car when he salvaged Maserati from bankruptcy, but he knew there was a market for a large luxury saloon with sporting overtones – something the first Quattroporte had demonstrated.

De Tomaso's Quattroporte, the III

So as De Tomaso was planning his entry into the luxury small car market with the Biturbo, he put into production the Berlina Quattroporte, *tipo* AM 330, known now as the QP III.

It had been seen in prototype form at the Turin show in 1976, soon after De Tomaso took over Maserati, but its official launch was at Turin three years later in 1979 – and it went into production in 1980, marking the return of the V8 engine to production after the unfortunate flirtation with a French mistress.

The sporting heritage was certainly hammered home in the launch brochure, which

Giugiaro's design was built by Ital, trimmed and painted at Innocenti and finished mechanically at Modena. It sold well, providing a valuable cash flow in the Biturbo's early years. (Fonte Archivio Maserati)

invoked the names not only of the traditional heroes of the marque – Nuvolari, Varzi, Farina, Fangio and Ascari – but also Moss, Hawthorn, Surtees and Wilbur Shaw. They were listed in that order, Latins first.

The big, flexible 4.2-litre unit that had appeared in the first Quattroporte now put out 255bhp at 6,000rpm with a maximum torque of 260lb ft (36kg m) at 3,000rpm, and the 4.9-litre engine 280bhp at 5,600rpm and maximum torque of 290lb ft (40kg m) at 3,000rpm. There was enough torque there to idle along in top gear in heavy traffic.

The 4.2 had the five-speed ZF gearbox and the 4.9-litre, aimed primarily at the American market, came with the Chrysler three-speed automatic transmission to a conventional differential.

Steering was power assisted, braking servo-assisted and there was independent suspension all round. *Car* magazine, in an unusually obscurantist aside, noted that it did not have ABS, which it thought did not matter. 'If your car has good balance and weight distribution, you don't need it. We tested it in 1976 and found it expensive and complex.' Maserati presumably thought the same at that stage.

It was heavy (over 2 tons) and very large – 16ft 5in (4,980mm) long, 5ft 10in (1,790mm) wide and 4ft 5in (1,350mm) high, with a wheelbase of 9ft 2in (2,800mm) – but the design by Giorgetto Giugiaro cunningly concealed its bulk. The bonnet was long and imposing, the boot huge, and the rubber inserts built into the bumpers to meet US crash regulations were not obtrusive, as they were in the botched conversions of many other cars.

In outline it was a vague wedge and one of its main markets was the Middle East – for which many cars were finished in white with white interiors. The unit-construction bodies were built by Ital Design, then trimmed and painted at the Innocenti works in Milan and finished mechanically at Modena. By 1982, production was two a day.

This was a car for the very rich or very powerful who expected the ultimate in luxury, like Sandro Pertini, president of Italy between 1978 and 1985. There is a tale that the car that De Tomaso provided for him failed to start on its maiden trip, leading to specially built Lancia Flavia limousines being used instead.

The Quattroporte's seating was Italian leather, naturally, and air conditioning, controlled from a wood-veneered centre console, came as standard. The dashboard was rectangular and very similar to the one that was to appear in the first Biturbos. Another feature that was to be repeated was the appearance of a stylized trident on the fuel filler cap.

De Tomaso's decision to make an Italian flagship was soon vindicated. Orders flowed in from 1980 – it sold 120 in Italy alone that year – and provided valuable cash flow as the Biturbo was being developed.

Even so, it was probably still underpriced for a large, hand-built car. It was actually cheaper than the Kyalami, which shared its 4.2 and 4.9 engines: in 1984, the 4.9 Quattroporte was the Italian equivalent of £22,700, the Kyalami with the same engine was £25,000. But in the next few years the cost went rocketing up.

The Quattroporte III was a competitor for the large British Jaguars and for the Mercedes S-Class W126, which made its debut in the same year. Mercedes was wont to say of the S-Class, 'You don't simply decide to buy an S-Class: it comes to you when fate has ordained that your life should take that course.'

People who bought a Quattroporte did so because they really wanted to, rather than waiting for mystic signs from Germany. Another competitor from the mid-1980s was the Bentley Turbo R; the earlier, disappointing, Bentley T series was a Rolls-Royce clone and not to be considered in the same breath.

America, which took the bulk of Quattroporte sales, had models fitted with four special catalysers to meet emissions requirements, which knocked maximum speed down to about 123mph (198km/h). When *Road & Track* tested one, they noted that it was the least fuel-efficient car in America, getting only 8mpg on the EPA city cycle: 'Every time you step onto the gas, you can sense ten-dollar bills spewing out of the exhaust pipe.'

The Royale

On 14 December 1986, the Quattroporte III was replaced by an even more luxurious model, the Royale. This was a prestige-by-association link with the name used by Bugatti when he created his 12.0-litre monster limousine in 1930, notionally to be sold only to members of royal families – though it is said

The lines of De Tomaso's Quattroporte were softened for the Royale, interior materials were of even higher quality and it was claimed that running was absolutely silent. (Nicholas Colquhoun-Denvers)

(Nicholas Colquhoun-Denvers)

that Ettore refused to sell one to King Zog of Albania because of his table manners.

What enthusiasts tend to cite as the height of decadence when talking about the Berlina Royale, as the factory styled it, are the fridge/bar (though this was not standard), the storing of pewter goblets behind the centre door pillars and the retractable rosewood tables in the doors, on which the goblets could be placed. As usual, there was the finest hand-crafted leather seating with extra padding.

But there were other more important changes to the car: there was an electric sunroof and new hubcaps on the existing wheels. The facia and cabin were furnished with higher quality materials and when the doors were opened at night, lights shone onto the road so that the pampered occupants would not step

Presidents of republics and captains of industry could sip from goblets on walnut tables in the Royale, as they were propelled at speeds of up to 140mph (225km/h). (Nicholas Colquhoun-Denvers)

into puddles. On the boot the word 'Royale' appeared.

Power went up as the compression ratio in the 4.9-litre engine was increased to 9.5:1, which gave 300bhp at 5,600rpm. This allowed the Royale to be hustled along at a maximum of 143mph (230km/h), an astonishing speed for a car weighing 4,272lb (1,938kg).

Much was spent on acoustic insulation, giving 'absolutely silent running', according to the model's press release. The cost was twice that of a 430; it Italy in 1988 it was the equivalent of £58,000.

The bulk of Quattroporte III production was up to the mid-1980s; after that the Royale was really built only to special order and only fifty-one or fifty-two were made. The name has subsequently been used for far less distinguished vehicles by Vauxhall and Oldsmobile.

Production ceased in 1990/91 after a total of 2,155 models, including Royales. No right-hand-drive versions appear to have been available. By that time, Maserati had pulled out of their crucial American market because of quality and reliability problems, and the Quattroporte was not seen in America again until the fifth generation appeared there in 2004.

Quattroporte III + Royale (1975–90)

4.2 V8 engine	
Type	AM107.21.42
Layout	V8 90 degrees – 2 valves per cylinder, double overhead cam per bank
Bore × stroke:	88 × 85mm
Capacity:	4136cc
Compression ratio:	8.5:1
Max power:	255bhp/190.2kW@6,000rpm
Fuel system:	4 Weber 42 DCNF carburettors
Intercoolers:	None
4.9 V8 engine	
Type	AM107.23.49
Layout	V8 90 degrees – 2 valves per cylinder, double overhead cam per bank
Bore × stroke:	93.9 × 89mm
Capacity:	4930cc
Compression ratio:	8.5:1
Max power:	280bhp/208.8kW@5,600rpm (Royale: 300bhp/223.8kW@5,600rpm)
Fuel system:	4 Weber 42 DCNF carburettors
Intercoolers:	None
Transmission	
Gearbox:	Chrysler automatic 3-speed + reverse; manual option
Final drive:	Sensitork 3.07:1
Suspension	
Front:	Independent, coil springs, shock absorbers
Rear:	Independent, coil springs, shock absorbers, anti-roll bar
Steering:	Power-assisted rack and pinion
Brakes:	Servo-assisted
Running gear	
Wheels:	7½K × 15
Tyres:	215/70VR15 Royale – 225/70VR15
Performance	
Max speed:	148mph (238km/h)
Acceleration:	0–69mph (100km/h) in 6.5sec
Dimensions	
Wheelbase:	110.2in (2,800mm)
Front track:	59.8in (1,520mm)
Rear track:	59.8in (1,520mm)
Length:	193.3in (4,910mm)
Width:	74.4in (1,890mm)
Height:	54.5in (1,385mm)
Weight:	4,273lb (1,938kg)
Number built	2,155

13 The V8 Shamal and the Fiat connection

> The V8 is sublime … pure Latin magic.
>
> *Fast Lane*

The Shamal, named after a hot Middle Eastern wind, was the last car of the era when De Tomaso was in total control of Maserati. It was conceived in 1989, just before worsening financial circumstances forced him to sell 49 per cent of his Maserati stock and 55 per cent of his Innocenti holding to Fiat.

Worldwide sales had fallen from 6,000 in 1984 to fewer than 3,000 in 1989. In Britain, for instance, only 136 cars were registered in 1988 and 151 in 1989. The American market had virtually disappeared due to the Biturbo's quality problems – indeed, the Shamal was

never sold there, even though plans had been made to market it at around $85,000 in 1992, but by then Maserati had quit America.

At the launch of the Shamal, which was sold alongside its predecessor, the Karif, De Tomaso admitted that the firm's accumulated losses were 346bn lire (£170m). Help was at hand from Fiat, who had just failed to beat General Motors in the race to buy Saab.

De Tomaso needed capital, Fiat needed his factory at Lambrate in Milan. It had a capacity of 50,000 units a year, but was producing only 3,000 Maseratis and 12,000 Innocentis. Fiat's strategy was to buy existing manufacturing capacity rather than build new – it was cheaper and quicker – and move production of the Polish-built 126, the Panda and an Alfa model to Lambrate.

It cost Fiat only £58 million for their 49 per cent stake and for that they got the factory, 500 dealers, the Innocenti brand name and some Daihatsu products made in Italy. The deal suited De Tomaso as he got a cash injection and was left in control of Maserati with his 51 per cent – largely because Fiat did not want at this stage to be seen to monopolize the Italian car industry, having taken over Alfa Romeo a few years earlier.

The Shamal was the most aggressive of the Biturbo line so far, and De Tomaso liked to think of it as a return to Maserati's supercar heritage. It was announced in mock-up form on 14 December 1989, at the traditional pre-Christmas news conference, and did not go into production for another year.

To create the Shamal, Maserati put a hand-built aluminium 3217cc V8 engine into a Biturbo chassis. It was clear what market they were aiming for as the Spanish brochure described it as being *abiertamente su filiosophia de 'muscle car'*, though the English version avoided this phrase, saying that the body design 'aggressively states its sporting heritage'.

The hint of chrome on the black trapezoidal grille was 'the only concession to tradition in a strictly sports/racing package'. The front end looked much more modern than the rest of the range, the usual four square headlamps being replaced with one square and one round lamp either side of the grille.

The spoiler under the windscreen was later carried through on the Ghibli.

The lower spoiler assembly could be removed to allow the engine to be taken out from the front.

Projector beam lights

These were the so-called polyellipsoidal 'projector beam' lamps, designed in the late 1960s by the American lighting company Sylvania for General Motors. They were ideal for fast driving when low beams lacked range, as they produced a wide, flat beam without causing dazzle.

The bonnet had two distinctive air ducts either side. In black, the car exuded a certain menace, though the interior was the usual luxurious package, with hand-stitched leather seats, tinted glass, central locking, air conditioning and electric windows and mirrors. There was Alcantara on the doors and roof. The radio was still an extra.

It was designed by the Maserati Design Centre in conjunction with Marcello Gandini, who had drawn the Quattroporte II while at Bertone. Gandini said he wanted the car to look significantly different from the rest of the range, but failed to convince *Car* magazine, which declared that it was yet another Biturbo derivative.

Gandini was hampered by the fact that there was a lack of funds for a completely new car, so the Shamal was built on the floorpan of the Spyder, as had been the Karif before it, with a wheelbase of 7ft 10½in (2,400mm), though it was slightly longer and 5½in wider (140mm) than the Karif.

It was also vastly more expensive: in Italy in 1991 it cost more than 126m lira (£57,700), compared with the Karif's 71m (£32,600). In the UK in 1992 it retailed at £63,450, but came down to £58,200 the following year.

It was still a small car, only slightly larger than a Ford Escort, but a striking two-door

Gandini and the Maserati Design Centre put a distinctive bulge in the car's rear quarters.

Seven-spoke OZ alloys were standard; the hub cap was lockable.

coupé with thick central roof pillars that formed a roll-over bar. It made it look as if the roof was removable, which it was not. There was an unusual front spoiler beneath the windscreen and raised boot, which hinted at a spoiler without actually being one.

The most notable body features were the exaggerated side skirts and the rear wheel arches, which were flared out at the sides, with the top line of the arches kicking up at the back – a Gandini trademark in his later models.

It was not to everyone's taste. *Car* magazine called its looks 'different, but not good … chunky but hardly elegant'. Another writer, George Kacher in *Automobile Magazine*, called it a genuinely ugly car: 'But like the hunchback of Notre Dame or the Werewolf of London, it has a friendly heart.' *Fast Lane* said it looked like a 1970s Toyota.

The front grille was black, smaller than before and trimmed with chrome and a large trident. The Italian brochure pointed out, '*Il "family feeling" è assicurato dalla mascherina trapezoidale assai ridotta in altezza, caratterizzata da una griglia near …*' – 'The "family feeling" is assured by the trapezioidal grille, reduced in height and characterized by a black grid …'.

Beneath it, the front bumper assembly contained another black grille, housing four square fog and spot lights. Removing this assembly allowed the engine to be taken out from the front rather than being hoisted out of its compartment, as the subframe with the twin low-set air-to-air intercoolers and radiator could be pulled forwards. The wheels were 16in, seven-spoke OZ alloys, with the wheel nuts hidden behind lockable hub caps.

The V8 engine

The Shamal saw a Maserati V8 used for the first time with twin turbos. The engine was essentially an extra two cylinders tacked onto the V6

Maserati used twin turbochargers for the first time in a V8, generating a huge 325bhp.

Each bank of cylinders had a separate engine management system, which was claimed to allow the car to proceed on four cylinders if one bank failed.

Twin exhausts exited though the heavy rear bumper.

that had stood the Biturbo in such good stead. It was a 3217cc light alloy unit with the same 90-degree angle between the banks, which had a bore and stroke of 80mm, four valves per cylinder and four overhead camshafts.

It produced a huge 326bhp (239kW) at 6,000rpm and massive torque of 318lb ft (44kg m) at 2,800rpm. It had two new-generation, liquid-cooled turbochargers and Weber-Marelli fuel injection. Each bank of cylinders had a separate engine management system with an interface between them: theoretically, the car would proceed even if one of the systems failed.

There was even one prototype version that allowed a driver in heavy traffic to switch off one bank of cylinders for economy reasons and drive on half the engine. 'Unfortunately the mechanism proved to lack development work, or had some engineering defect as it left me stranded on the road with sparks and flame from the engine', recalls Bruno Alfiere in the Maserati *Catalogue Raisoneé*. Transmission to the Ranger 3.36:1 limited slip differential was through a Getrag 6-speed + reverse gearbox, which was also used in the BMW 850.

Factory figures – never to be completely relied upon – put the 0–62mph (100km/h) at 5.3sec and the top speed at 168mph (270km/h). Despite the huge speed and vast cost of the car, ABS was available only as an extra.

Four-position electronic suspension appeared for the first time on the Shamal. Like the Karif, it was built on the floorpan of the Spyder, but it looked a great deal more menacing.

Compare this with a new entrant into the twin-turbo market, the Alpina B10 of 1989, based on the BMW 535i. It had a six-cylinder in-line engine with twin Garrett T5 turbos and was claimed to be the fastest production saloon in the world. It put out 500bhp, reached 180mph (289km/h) and did 0–62mph in 5.2sec.

New electronic suspension

Maserati installed electronic suspension on the Shamal. The mechanics were the standard MacPherson strut at the front and trailing arms at the rear, though these were tubular rather than the usual pressed steel, but the major innovation was the computer-controlled suspension by Koni with four different levels of ride.

As the 16in wheels – seven-spoke alloys with a centre nut or overstyled OZ wheels – encountered bumps in the road, sensors on each shock absorber sent a message within 300 milliseconds to a central computer, which then adjusted the damping rate.

A button on the console next to the gear-lever allowed the driver to select one of four settings from very soft to very hard; the publicity characterized them like this:

1. Very soft for low speed and maximum comfort.
2. For speeds up to 100mph (160km/h).
3. The best setting for driveability, manageability, road-holding and comfort.
4. The perfect setting for drivers who like to maximize the sporting soul of the car.

After the engine was switched off, the setting defaulted to position 2 for restarting.

What's it like to drive?

However, this new configuration seemingly failed to tame the wayward nature of the Biturbo chassis, with several testers continuing to report vicious tailslides.

'On a good day the Shamal will storm from 0–60mph in 5.1sec', reported George Kacher for *Automobile Magazine* in 1992. 'On a bad day, however, the fat Michelin 245/45ZR-16 rear tyres will spin furiously, clouding the car's rear end in expensive blue smoke.' In the rain, weight distribution felt like 90/10, he claimed.

Nevertheless, he reported that the free-revving V8 put the Shamal on the same desirability scale as a Ferrari 348: 'The 348 may be

Shamals and more than eighty other Maseratis parade through Rome after a celebrity tour to mark Maserati's ninetieth anniversary in 2004. (Adam Painter)

Back in Modena … Shamals in the piazza for the Maserati ninetieth celebrations. (Adam Painter)

Shamal two-door coupé (1988–91)

Engine	
Type	AM479
Layout	V8 90 degrees – 4 valves per cylinder, double overhead cam per bank, two IHI turbochargers
Bore × stroke:	80 × 80mm
Capacity:	3217cc
Compression ratio:	7.5:1
Max power:	326bhp/239kW@6,000rpm
Max torque:	318lb ft/44kg m@2,800rpm
Fuel system:	Weber Marelli injection
Intercoolers:	2 air-to-air
Transmission	
Gearbox:	Getrag manual 6 speed + reverse
Final drive:	Ranger 3.36:1
Suspension	
Front:	MacPherson strut with anti-roll bar, coil springs, shock absorbers
Rear:	Tubular trailing arms, coil springs, shock absorbers, anti-roll bar; optional electronic control
Steering:	Power-assisted rack and pinion
Brakes:	Servo-assisted twin circuit, front and rear ventilated discs with floating calipers, rear drum parking brake
Running gear	
Wheels:	8J × 16 (front), 9J × 16 (rear)
Tyres:	225/45 ZR-16 MXX (front) 245/45 ZR-16 MXX (rear)
Performance	
Max speed:	168mph (270km/h)
Acceleration:	0–62mph(100km/h) in 5.3sec
Dimensions	
Wheelbase:	94.5in (2,400mm)
Front track:	59.5in (1,512mm)
Rear track:	61in (1,550mm)
Length:	161.4in (4,100mm)
Width:	72.8in (1,850mm)
Height:	51.2in (1,300mm)
Weight	3,124lb (1,417kg)
Number built	369

a better car, but the Shamal is weirder, badder, quicker, even more exotic and ultimately more fun to drive.'

In Britain in 1992, it cost a little bit more than a Porsche Carrera RS. 'With a Maserati', said *Fast Lane*, 'you are paying for handmade Italian opulence, a simply great name steeped in nostalgia and heritage and, of course, exclusivity.'

Fast Lane was very impressed with the lack of turbo lag and the seamless delivery of power up to 6,000rpm, but couldn't hear the V8 burble, only a terrific turbo whistle. 'It's easy to drive fast; it doesn't demand or reward, like a 911 does.'

The Shamal was in limited production for only three years and 369 were built before it ended in 1994, though it was still being catalogued in the UK in September 1995 at £54,995.

14 The Ghibli

The last – and probably the best – of the line that could be traced back directly to the first Biturbos was the Ghibli – the original wedge now smoothed and curved even further by the Maserati design centre.

The Biturbo's reputation of being fast but fragile was finally seen off by this desirable, well-built, much-improved model: 'It has what BMW M3s and front-engined Porsches and the Japanese stopwatch specials lack: character, soul and personality', declared *Car*.

It appeared at the Turin motor show in April 1992, a year before an enfeebled De Tomaso sold out completely to Fiat, and it revived the

The new Ghibli of the 1990s, sometimes called the Ghibli II, was a worthy successor to the car that gave it its name, Giugiaro's two-seater coupé that ran from 1967 to 1973.

name of one of Maserati's most successful cars, the V8 Ghibli of 1967 to 1972, which sold in both coupé and Spyder form. For this reason it is sometimes known as the Ghibli II. While the confusing range of Maserati models had been reduced to two by 1992 – the Ghibli and the Spyder – the Ghibli itself appeared under a plethora of names.

Production ran, with a short break, up until 1999 and the cars got better and better as the quality improved. Early Ghiblis suffered from corrosion, but rust-proofing and general build quality was improved in later models, largely due to the efforts of Dott. Ing. Eugenio Alzati, installed by Fiat as Maserati's managing director in 1993, with a remit to upgrade the final cars of the De Tomaso era, the Ghibli and Quattroporte.

Inside there were the usual Maserati luxury fittings, including leather trim, climate control,

By the time the last of the line, the Ghibli, appeared the reputation of the Biturbo derivatives being fast but fragile was beginning to disappear. Everyone agreed that they were sweet-handling cars. The tubular rear lower wishbones came from the Shamal and Ghibli Open Cup and the rear axle from the new Quattroporte via Ferrari. (LAT)

central locking and power-operated seat backs. However, it did lack side impact bars, an airbag and anti-lock brakes – *Autocar* thought this 'scandalous' for a car that they got up to 153mph (246km/h).

Ghiblis garnered enthusiastic reviews. The Dutch car magazine *Autovisie* tested a Ghibli once and described its handling in traffic as being as speedy as a 'rat in the sewers'.

As Giancarlo Perini put it in *Car*, 'The idea of 300bhp-plus from 2.0 litres sounds like an over-seasoned bowl of pasta – tempting, but not something you'd want every day. Yet the Ghibli is very habitable and refined, almost sober in some ways.'

The body details did not alter during the life of the car, except for the deletion of the dummy fuel-filler on the left-hand rear wing in 1995.

The Serie 1

The first Ghibli had a 2.0-litre engine only, and had a distributor and an early version of the fuel injection system – similar to the 2.24/222 4v. The first set of revisions occurred in 1993, which saw the introduction of the 2.8 version that came to the UK, by which time all versions had deleted the distributor.

UK tests of the 2.8 showed it had a maximum of 153mph (246kph)at 5,840rpm and a 0–60mph (96.5km/h) time of 5.6sec. The top speed was 10mph (16km/h) down on the factory claims.

The 2.0-litre engine for the Italian market turned out 306bhp at 6,250rpm and 276lb ft of torque. It was not brought into Britain as the importers did not think anyone would pay more than £35,000 for a 2.0-litre car. *Autocar* disagreed; its tester Andrew Frankel reported:

> Its punch is extraordinary. A day at Goodwood with the entire Maserati range confirmed it to be a better car than even the mighty V8 Shamal. The engine is smooth, incredibly flexible given its small capacity, and soaked in torque. I found you could balance it through Goodwood's fiendishly tricky corners with a precision and confidence I cannot remember from another turbo car.

It was a bit of a screamer – the rev-limiter was said to be 6,750rpm, 500rpm higher than the softer export edition of 2.8 litres, which had 25bhp less and cost £42,000 in the UK. Nevertheless it produced 320lb ft of torque, enabling a claimed time of 5.6sec from 0 to 60mph (96.5km/h) and a top speed of more than 163mph (262km/h).

One significant mechanical difference between them was that the 2.0-litre had aluminium cylinder liners, while the 2.8's were cast iron. Both were, of course, developed from previous 222 and 430 Biturbo range and had a new engine management system with a separate control unit for each bank of cylinders, and with electronic ignition.

The body shape was yet another smoothed-out version of the Biturbo bodyshell, still with pairs of rectangular headlights and a steeply sloping bonnet line with ducts and a large rear end, which, according to Maserati, 'essentially interprets the considerable power being transmitted to the rear axle'.

Brakes were servo-assisted (ABS was still to arrive), the gearbox was a Getrag five-speed transmitting the power to a cooled Ranger differential. The cooler went where the spare wheel was normally placed, so this was deleted and canisters of inflating foam for punctured tyres were supplied instead. A four-speed ZF automatic was available on the 2.8.

Ghibli UK prices 1996

Ghibli manual	£44,931
Ghibli auto	£45,979
Ghibli GT manual	£47,549
Ghibli GT auto	£48,662

NB The Kit Sportivo, which had to be ordered from the factory on a new car, was a £1,733 option. Active Ride suspension was £998.75

Despite the number plate, it's not a Cup but a Ghibli MY94, manufactured in May that year and imported from Italy in 1998. It originally had 16in Merak-style alloy wheels, but these were changed for the 17in Speedline split rim wheels used on the Ghibli Cup. (Enrico)

The MY94

There seems to have been no Serie 2, as the model now became designated the MY94 – representing the Model Year. Sometimes ABS is added to the name to mark, at last, the introduction of Bosch four-sensor ABS. There were also side impact bars in the doors and, like all injected cars, an inertia switch on the fuel feed system to stop fuel spills in the case of an accident. Confusingly, the MY94 did not appear in the UK until 1995.

The MY95

Ghibli GT specification, with a Getrag six-speed gearbox, which had been available on 2.0-litre home market cars much earlier.

The K.S. 95

This stood for *Kit Sportivo* – the ride height was lowered by 3/4in (20mm) and there were heavier roll bars at the front and rear. The tyres were larger and the OZ Futura alloy wheels

The Ghibli GT, which ran from 1995 to the end of production, had new seven-spoke alloys – these are Mille Miglias, though OZ versions were also available. There was also a driver's airbag.

were 17in, rather than the 16in magnesium alloy on the previous models, which had shown that it was rather too easy for the catalytic converter to hit the tarmac. The *Kit Sportivo* could be ordered from the factory on a new car, or a kit of parts could be bought later and fitted by a Maserati dealer.

The Ghibli GT

Also produced from the 1995 model year, in 2.0-litre and 2.8-litre forms, was the GT, 'embodying the finest traditions of the Italian Grand Turismo', as the brochure put it.

It had some styling tweaks and new 17in seven-spoke alloys, made by both OZ and Mille Miglia. Like all Ghiblis and Shamals, it had the spoiler beneath the windscreen to increase wiper adhesion at speed. The backing for the one-piece headlamps changed from silver to black.

The pressed steel rear suspension was replaced with tubular rear lower wishbones, as used in the Shamal and Ghibli Open Cup, and the rear axle came from the new Quattroporte via Ferrari. The four-position electronic suspension was an extra. This was the version that continued in production until replaced by the 3200 coupé.

The Chubasco

It is worth recalling that as the De Tomaso era drew to an end, there was one exciting design exercise that came to nothing, and two attempts to return Maserati to its racing heritage.

The design exercise, which appeared in 1990 at De Tomaso's traditional December presentation, was the Chubasco – named after a Californian wind. It was a sleek two-seater, mid-engined car with innovative suspension and characterized by its central backbone chassis, as used in many of De Tomaso's own cars since the Vallelunga of 1964.

Its dramatic appearance, albeit in mock-up guise, stole the thunder of the two production cars that were being previewed, the Racing and the Shamal.

Low, red and sleek, the Chubasco had a large, electrically controlled glass sunroof that moved back and over the engine compartment, and there was a huge aerofoil at the rear. The doors were single-hinged in front and opened upwards and to the front.

As it was designed by Marcello Gandini it had his traditional kick-up on the rear wheel arches. But it was only a static prototype – the only one Maserati ever demonstrated – despite the press notice claiming:

- It is a coupé but also an aggressive roadster.
- It is an F1 car with air con.
- It is an extremely high performance machine.

It is said that Maserati had decided that it was too expensive to make even before it was unveiled, though there had been talk of it appearing in limited production form in 1992 with the 430bhp V8 engine from the Shamal. A tantalizing reminder of what might have been, the Chubasco remains in its mock-up form in the excellent Panini museum on the outskirts of Modena.

The Barchetta

Exactly a year later, De Tomaso presented a rather more practical car, designed to appeal to that mythic beast the 'gentleman driver' and to be used for one-make racing. This was the Barchetta, or 'little boat', a name used by Ferrari in the 1950s and by Fiat in the 1990s.

It built on the experience of the Chubasco chassis, this time with the same type of central backbone made of aluminium and composite materials. It had a Ghibli 2.0-litre 316bhp engine with roller bearing turbos, mounted behind the driver and ahead of a six-speed ZF transaxle. Wheels were Marchesini 18in alloys.

The body was made of a mixture of aluminium honeycomb, carbon fibre and fibreglass layers. There was a central tub and removable shrouds over the front and rear of the chassis. Three longitudinal tubes protruding forwards from the front subframe carried the nose in factory drawings but not in reality. As it was open-topped and extremely light, top speed was more than 185mph (300km/h).

De Tomaso's plan was to build twenty-five Barchetta Corsa competition cars, but only seventeen were ever built, which took part in sixteen races in 1992 and 1993. A detuned road-going version, the Stradale, with lights, indicators and other essentials for road use was also planned, but it is unclear whether any ever made it on to the streets. A handful of the competition cars have since been adapted for road use.

Looking forward to the 1993 British motor show, *Autocar* reported:

> The biggest eye-catcher will be the Barchetta, displayed in one-make racer form but almost indistinguishable on the surface and under the skin from its road-going equivalent. It's every bit as good and fast to drive as it looks.

Certainly there was an attempt to homologate the car in Britain for low-volume type approval the previous year. Much work was done at Church Green Engineering outside Shaftesbury, in Dorset. Anthony Cazalet recalls taking the car to MIRA for crash testing – the only requirement at that time being that in a crash the steering wheel did not obtrude further into the cabin:

> When it ran into the concrete, the whole car pivoted around some longitudinal tubes at the front – the back went up in the air and then the whole thing crashed down to the ground virtually destroying the car – but because the steering wheel had not moved it passed the test!

This car had already been crash-tested in Italy, so led a hard life. It was probably unique in having Fiat coupé headlamps faired into the wings.

The project was hugely expensive and probably collapsed under the weight of its costs, though conspiracy theorists maintain that Fiat – now completely in the driving seat after the demise of De Tomaso – cancelled it because it was perceived as a threat to Ferrari.

The Open Cup

Early sales of the Ghibli were not up to expectations, probably because the improvements had not been sufficient to generate enthusiasm – the basic shape, did, after all, go back some twelve years and competition from the German sporting saloons was intense.

A rare piece of post-war Maserati racing history – a Ghibli Open Cup, one of the twenty-five constructed for the Maserati Open Cup championship series in the mid-1990s. This is the ex-Duncan Huisman car, which took pole position in both the 1996 races, but failed to finish. (Claus Müller)

So to generate interest – and sales – Fiat fell back on the time-honoured manufacturer's trick of going to the races with a modified production car, rather than creating a unique racer like the Barchetta. This was a much more serious attempt at competition, with a car that could be used on the track and then converted easily by the factory to road use.

The standard 2.0-litre Ghibli, with the four-valve V6 engine and six-speed Getrag gearbox, was heavily modified by Alfa Corse, with a roll cage, Sparco racing seat, a five-point seat belt, slick tyres, automatic fire system and fireproof linings in the doors. The engine had improvements to breathing and fuel injection, and roller bearing turbos. Maximum power at the outset was 320bhp at 6,500rpm.

Again, it was to be a one-marque racing series, in conjunction with the DTM, entitled the Selenia Ghibli Open Cup (Selenia was then part of Fiat's lubricants division, but is now American-owned). It was organized by Dott. Adolfo Orsi of Historica Selecta, a scion of the Orsi family who had once owned Maserati.

Drivers bought the car for around £48,000 and for an additional £9,000 they could take part – all expenses paid, including tyres – in eight races in the 1995 season on eight circuits in Europe, two in Italy. 'Both professional drivers and gentlemen, holders of a FIA international licence A or B, may participate', according to the regulations. The best professional and the best gentleman in the final classification received 30m lira each. The best lady would have got 15m.

The first Cup event was at Imola at the end of April 1995 and the last at Magny Cours in October. The winner in the amateur class at the end of this first season was twenty-year-old Denny Zardo (Zara Automobili) with 118 points, well ahead of Federico D'Amore (Mocauto) in the professional class, with 103 points. What was notable was the reliability of the Open Cup and its fearsome performance, with a maximum speed of 167mph (269km/h) and a 0–60mph (96km/h) of 4.1sec.

For the following year, substantial changes were made to the specifications, including rose-jointed suspension and 18in wheels with larger discs and calipers (to answer criticisms of the brakes) and modifications to subframes, the exhaust system, headlamps, spoilers and even the gear stick.

This upgrading resulted in the lighter Ghibli Open Cup Evoluzione for the 1996 season of races at eight circuits. Power was now officially 330bhp, but it was rumoured that 350bhp could now be squeezed out of the engine, which, like the gearbox and differential, was sealed by Maserati before delivery so that only routine maintenance was possible.

The 1996 series came to an end abruptly after two races, at Monza in March and Jarama in April. Fiat maintained that the cost/benefit ratio was not good enough to keep the series going. More meat here for the conspiracists, who say that the new Evo was quicker on the track than the Ferrari 355 Challenge, which Maranello could not countenance.

There's some slight doubt as to how many Open Cups were built, as sources put the number between twenty-two and twenty-seven, but it is probably in the region of twenty-five; certainly twenty-one of them took part in the 1995 series, according to Adolfo Orsi.

Confusion arises further as there appear to be a few cars that have been converted from a standard Ghibli version to Open Cups by using new or used spares. (Three cars were written off in the 1996 season.) An Open Cup engine rebuilt by Maserati was offered in 2005 for €13,000 and two new Sparco seats for €900 each. After the races most Open Cups were converted for street use – eight of them in Germany in 1997.

The Ghibli Cup

The first year's Open Cup series, ending in October 1995, had achieved great success in demonstrating the Ghibli's capabilities and convinced Maserati that the range could be stretched by building on the Open Cup's reputation with a limited-edition road-going version, entitled the Ghibli Cup. It appeared first at the Bologna motor show in December of 1995 and was described by Maserati as a 'direct descendant of the Ghibli Open Cup'.

It appeared only with a 2.0-litre engine, even in the right-hand-drive versions, and delivered the same output as the early competition car of 330bhp at 6,750rpm, so was much more highly tuned than its standard 2-litre Ghibli sibling, which developed 306bhp at 6,250rpm. The improvement was achieved using a modified engine management system and redesigned exhaust.

Unlike any other road model, except for the Quattroporte Evoluzione, it used roller bearing turbos to cope with the boost needed to achieve 165bhp per litre – the highest output of any production car in the world.

The target market was Italy, for which a limited edition of fifty was produced at first. Maserati defined the putative buyer thus:

> The typical purchaser is in his thirties; a professional or entrepreneur who loves spirited driving; an enthusiast of energetic, agile cars of aggressive line, but at the same time elegant, well-finished and reliable.

What this exemplar got for his lira was what *Autocar* called 'The most highly-tuned road car

The doors on the Cup had carbon fibre, rather than wood, fillets.

The Cup's engine had a modified engine management system that boosted power to 330bhp at 6,750rpm – a huge output from a 2.0-litre engine.

Drilled Momo pedals were a feature of the Cup; there was also a Momo filler cap.

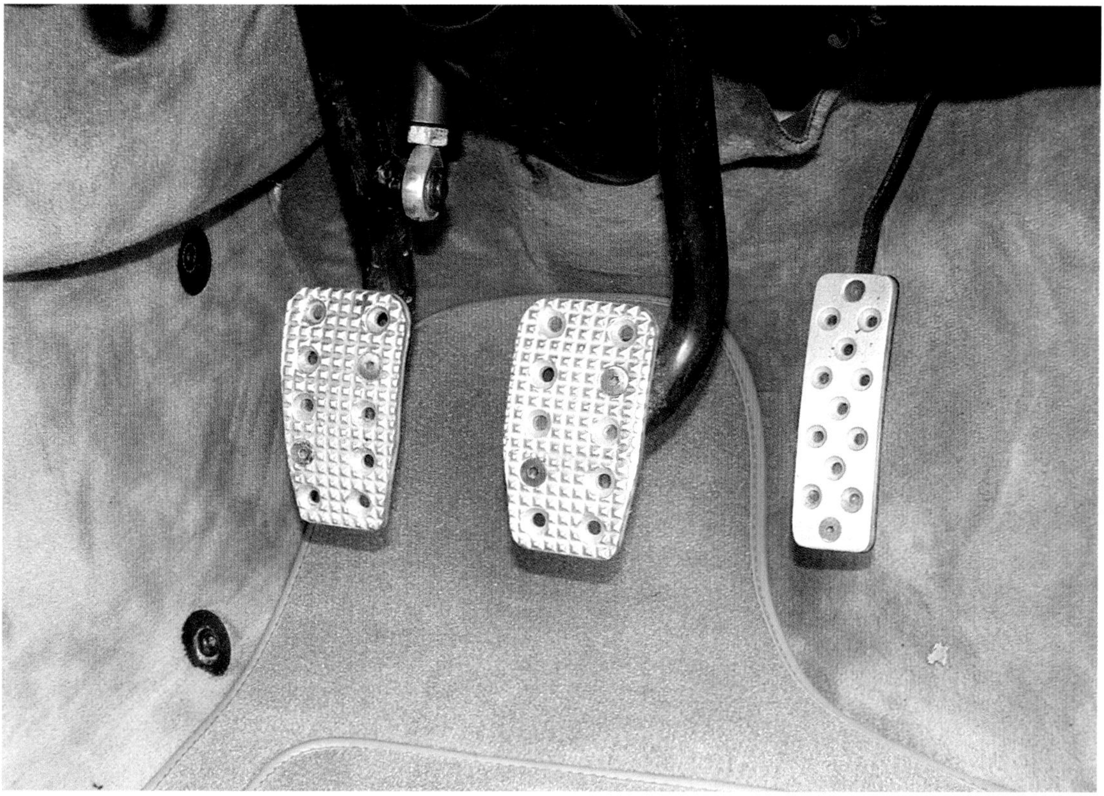

Performance comparison – Ghibli models

	Ghibli Cup	Ghibli 2.0	Ghibli 2.8
Engine size	1996cc	1996cc	2790cc
Max power	330bhp@6,750rpm	306bhp@6,250rpm	284bhp@6,000rpm
Max torque	273.4lb ft/37.8kg m @4,000rpm	274.8lb ft/38kg m @4,250rpm	304.5lb ft/42.1kg m @3,500rpm
Max speed	168mph (270km/h)	164mph (265km/h)	161mph (260km/h)
0–62mph (0–100km/h)	5.6sec	5.7sec	5.7sec

engine in production – a quad-camshaft 2.0-litre V6 that produces a scarcely credible 330bhp alongside 280lb/ft at 4,000rpm.' It described it, wrongly, as being the first new engine seen in a Maserati for two decades – which suggested that the magazine had failed to follow the development of the four-valve engine. It summarized the Cup as having an awful driving position and being 'a bit pricey', which indeed it was, but praised it for blistering performance and understated looks.

Top speed was 168mph (270km/h) and 0–62mph (0–100km/h) took 5.6sec, a favourite figure in Maserati publicity handouts, but this time probably justified.

In the basic metal, the Cup, 2.0-litre and 2.8 were identical and the mechanical specification, other than the engine, was the same. All had the Getrag six-speed gearbox, limited slip ZF differential of 3.45:1 (3.9:1 for the 2.8 with the option of four-speed ZF automatic transmission), electronic four-position suspension,

Twin Cups at a Maserati Club UK rally in wet North Wales.

Lowered suspension and 17in Speedline split-rim alloys distinguish the Cup from the Ghibli GT.

dual circuit brakes with drilled front discs, servo and ABS, and 17in wheel rims (16in on early Ghiblis).

But the Cup's Eibach springs were shorter and stiffer, and there were larger Brembo brakes with four-pot calipers and drilled discs.

There were also cosmetic touches to distinguish it, a Ghibli Open Cup badge on the lower doors, 17in Speedline alloys with five-spoke split rims, an aluminium filler cap and burnished tailpipes – a single outlet per side rather than two as in the other models.

Inside there was Connolly leather, a new Momo Corse leather steering wheel, the wooden fillets were replaced with carbon fibre, there were drilled aluminium pedals and, on the dash, left-hand-drive cars had a numbered identification plaque in silver underneath the radio. Exterior colours were metallic green, blue, black and grey.

The Cup cost £46,795 in the UK, exactly £3,000 more than the Ghibli GT. The four-speed automatic option on the GT was another £1,800.

Manufacturer's figures for 1995 suggested that the gap in performance between the Cup and the other models was not as great as might be thought, as shown in the table on p.148.

Some sixty of the 2.0-litre genuine Cups were made; there were also fifteen powered by the 2.8-litre V6, in its much milder state of tune. As *Performance Car* put it:

The Cup had single exhausts either side exiting though the rear bumper, rather than twin each side on the GT.

This Ghibli Cup engine has been used in a Barchetta.

The last Ghiblis were very difficult to sell as Maserati marketed them alongside the brand-new 3200 coupé by Giugiaro. (LAT)

Up for the Cup

Scot Crane bought his Ghibli Cup in 1999 when it was two years old and had 25,000 miles on the clock. It had previously been owned by the editor of *Evo* magazine and was – and still is – in immaculate condition. The only changes to the norm are Recaro seats and a straight-through exhaust, avoiding the catalyst, used on track days at Donington, Goodwood and Spa.

Scot does about 3,000–4,000 miles a year and loves the car, pointing out that it has a better bhp/ton ratio than the 2005 Maserati GranSport – and that has an engine more than twice the size. 'In these days of electronic everything – fly-by-wire throttles and ESPs – it's the last pure Maserati driver's car.'

Magically special moments come when you work harmoniously with the Cup, keeping the engine in the singing rev band, using the roadholding and handling to its best advantage, wallowing in the sheer excitement of the massive thrust of the engine.

Everyone who tested it loved it – *Performance Car* named it their coupé of the year for 1996. *Top Gear* magazine said, 'Its grip and suspension are best described as totally awesome.' *Autocar* talked of 'hyperspace third gear acceleration and fabulous traction'.

Some eighty-six Cups were made, and about twenty-five were imported into Britain; their present owners are devotees of this new religious order.

The Primatist

Maserati had been building engines for powerboats since the 1930s, their light alloy construction making them ideal for racing on the lakes of northern Italy. A notable record of 70.84mph (114km/h) was set on Lake Garda in 1933 by Count Theo Rossi of Montelera, using a 3.0-litre, eight-cylinder Maserati 8CM. Throughout the 1950s and 1960s Maserati-engined boats had many class wins in world and European championships.

The marine tradition was revived on Lake Lugano in November 1996, when Guido Cappellini set a new world record for the flying kilometre of 134.66mph (216.703km/h) in a Maserati-powered monocoque, built by Bruno Abbate's Cantiere Nautico Primatist outside Menaggio, on Lake Como. The engine tuners Romeo Ferraris, who offer several modifications for later Maseratis, marinized a 2.0-litre V6 from the Ghibli Cup to give a colossal 334bhp (248kW).

The Ghibli Primatist of 1997 was a limited edition to mark the achievement. It used the 2.0-litre, four-valve engine, but for road use producing rather less power – 306bhp at 6,250rpm. Some thirty-five were made.

All Primatists were finished in ultramarine. The interior was the same as the normal Ghibli, except that the blue leather seats were finished

with eye-wateringly bright turquoise trim, which carried through to the dash and around the console and doors. This turquoise, combined with the very light burr walnut of the steering wheel and dash inserts, make sitting in the Primatist a testing experience for the sensitive, though it was said to have been designed by naval furnishing experts.

The other identifying characteristic is the small Ghibli Primatist decals in front of the rear wheel arches. The 17in Allesio Speedline alloys from the Ghibli Cup were declared in the brochure to be an option. Electronic suspension was also an option.

The end of the line

The Ghibli was a highly regarded car that remained in series production until November 1997, when Maserati's new owners, Ferrari, gutted the factory at Viale Ciro Menotti and re-equipped with the most modern production facilities available.

It was time for another rebirth since, despite the Ghibli's success, production at Maserati had been dropping for a few years. Contrast this with the regularity of production of its new owners:

	Maserati	**Ferrari**
1995	1,000	3,307
1996	800	3,313
1997	500	3,581

After Ferrari reopened the factory in May 1998, some 250 or so Ghibli GTs were produced from left-over parts before production finally ended, with a total of more than 2,300 Ghiblis of all versions having been built. About seventeen of the Ferrari-made Ghiblis were imported into the UK. They can be distinguished by their high-level brake lights. The number that came in before the factory shut down was some 150 cars, including twenty-six Cup models.

The last Ghibli GTs, built after the factory re-opened, were the final and best evocation of a line that had begun nearly two decades earlier, but proved very difficult to sell, as Maserati were now concentrating on building a market for the new 3200 coupé, styled by Giorgetto Giugiaro's Italdesign to look radically different. Giugiaro was quoted as saying:

> It is the first Maserati to abandon the boxy look we have all known for years in a return to the softer lines we remember from the famous Maseratis of the firm's golden past.

The engine of one of the last Ghiblis made; the total was some 2,300, making it one of Maserati's best-sellers.

Specification for later versions of Ghibli/GT/Cup two-door coupé (1992–98)

Ghibli 2.0 engine

Type	AM496
Layout	V6 90 degrees – 4 valves per cylinder, double overhead cam per bank, two IHI turbo-chargers
Bore × stroke:	82 × 63mm
Capacity:	1992cc
Compression ratio:	7.6:1
Max power:	306bhp/228kW@5,500rpm
Max torque:	304lb ft/42.04kg m @4,250rpm
Fuel system:	Weber Marelli injection
Intercoolers:	2 air-to-air

Ghibli 2.8 Engine

Type	AM477
Layout	V6 90 degrees – 4 valves per cylinder, double overhead cam per bank, two IHI turbochargers
Bore × stroke:	94 × 67mm
Capacity:	2790cc
Compression ratio:	7.4:1
Max power:	284bhp/211kW@5,500rpm
Max torque:	304lb ft/42.04kg m @4,250rpm
Fuel system:	Weber Marelli injection
Intercoolers:	2 air-to-air

Ghibli Cup Engine

Type	AM496
Layout	V6 90 degrees – 4 valves per cylinder, double overhead cam per bank, two IHI turbo-chargers
Bore × stroke:	82 × 63mm
Capacity:	1992cc
Compression ratio:	7.6:1
Max power:	330bhp/246kW@6,750rpm
Max torque:	304lb ft/42.04kg m @4,000rpm
Fuel system:	Weber Marelli injection
Intercoolers:	2 air-to-air

Transmission

Gearbox:	Getrag 6-speed; opt ZF 4-speed auto (2.8)
Final drive:	ZF 3.45:1; 3.25:1 (2.8) 3.90:1 (auto)

Suspension

Type:	Independent, four-position electronic suspension
Steering:	Power-assisted rack and pinion with double gearing servo
Brakes:	Servo-assisted twin circuit

Running gear

Wheels:	8J × 17 (front), 9J × 17 (rear)
Tyres:	215/45 ZR17 (front), 245/40 ZR17 (rear)

Performance

Max speed:	164mph (265km/h) (2.0) 161mph (260km/h) (2.8) 168mph (270km/h) (Cup)
Acceleration	0–62mph (100km/h) in 5.7sec (2.0 & 2.8), 5.6sec (Cup)

Dimensions

Wheelbase:	99in (2,514mm)
Front track:	59.6in (1,515mm)
Rear track:	59.4in (1,510mm)
Length:	166.3in (4,223mm)
Width:	69.9in (1,775mm)
Height:	51.2in (1,300mm)
Weight:	3,009lb (1,365kg) (manual)

Number built 2,300

Since the end of production, Campana Carrozzeria of Modena, who have been involved with Maseratis since 1947, have offered Ghibli Cup owners glass-fibre body kits including side skirts, bumpers and front headlamp cowlings similar to the Karif's. They can, of course, also be fitted to the other Ghiblis of the same era.

Barchetta two-seat racer (1990–92)

Engine	
Type	AM501
Layout	V6 90 degrees – 4 valves per cylinder, double overhead cam per bank, two IHI turbochargers
Bore × stroke:	82 × 63.5mm
Capacity:	1996cc
Compression ratio:	7.8:1
Max power:	315bhp@6,000rpm
Fuel system:	Weber Marelli injection
Intercoolers:	2 air-to-air
Transmission	
Gearbox:	ZF six-speed transaxle
Suspension	
Front:	Double wishbones, with inboard coil over shock absorbers
Rear:	Double wishbones, with inboard coil over shock absorbers
Brakes	Dual circuit non-servo
Running gear	
Wheels:	18in
Tyres:	245/40 ZR 18 (front) 285/35 ZR 18 (rear)
Performance	
Max speed:	186mph (300km/h)
Dimensions	
Wheelbase:	102.4in (2,600mm)
Front track:	63.4in (1,610mm)
Rear track:	62.2in (1,580mm)
Length:	159.4in (4,050mm)
Width:	77 4in (1,965mm)
Height:	33.3in (845mm)
Weight	1,709lb (775kg)
Number built	17

Ghibli Open Cup one-marque racer (1995–96)

Engine	
Type	AM577
Layout	V6 90 degrees – 4 valves per cylinder, double overhead cam per bank, two IHI turbochargers
Bore × stroke:	82 × 63mm
Capacity:	1996cc
Compression ratio:	7.6:1
Max power:	330bhp/246kW@7,000rpm (some sources say 320bhp@6,500rpm)
Fuel system:	Weber Marelli injection
Intercoolers:	2 air-to-air
Transmission	
Gearbox:	Getrag 6-speed
Final drive:	ZF 3.45:1
Suspension	
Type:	Independent, MacPherson type, Eibach springs, Bilstein shock absorbers
Steering:	Power-assisted rack and pinion with double gearing servo
Brakes:	Servo-assisted drilled Brembo discs, four-pot calipers, twin circuit
Running gear	
Wheels:	8J × 17 (front) (18in front + rear in 1996), 9J × 17 (rear)
Tyres:	225/45 ZR17 (front) 245/40 ZR17 (rear)
Performance	
Max speed:	168mph (270km/h)
Dimensions	
Wheelbase:	98.8in (2,510mm)
Front track:	59.6in (1,515mm)
Rear track:	59.4in (1,510mm)
Weight:	2,800lb (1,270kg)
Number built	25

15 Fiat takes over and the Quattroporte IV

Aerodynamic, aggressive, but at the same time sober, refined and noble

Quattroporte brochure

The gossip from Modena in September 1989, according to *Autocar*, was that there was to be a new V8-engined car in which front-wheel drive was a distinct possibility! And there would be a new two-seater front-engined coupé, a variation on the Biturbo theme.

It would have been wise to take this with a pinch of salt. The two-seater did not appear, and when the new V8 eventually arrived as the Quattroporte IV nearly five years later it put its 335bhp through the rear axle as always.

After Royale production petered out, there was a three-year lull in the Quattroporte story until the successful Quattroporte IV appeared at the Turin motor show in April in 1994, a month after the launch of the Ghibli 94 at Geneva. The range now consisted of the Quattroporte with both V6 and V8 engines, the Ghibli, Spyder, Shamal and 430.

The Quattroporte was the fastest saloon in the luxury car sector and the first completely new car to appear after Fiat had gained full control of Maserati on 19 May 1993 and confirmed their intention of putting in resources to build the company up again. They had picked up the 51 per cent needed

Gandini's Quattroporte IV Evoluzione was constructed to Ferrari standards and was said to have 800 improved components compared with the previous model. One changed item was the Lasalle clock, replaced with a digital readout. (Fonte Archivio Maserati)

The Quattroporte IV was originally offered with the 2.0-litre V6, then the 2.8-litre V6 and then the V8.

for control from De Tomaso for a mere £33m; they had paid him £58m for the earlier 49 per cent.

The Innocenti factory at Lambrate, which had produced Biturbo bodyshells alongside the Innocenti Mini, was closed despite union protests and Maserati bodies were now built at Golden Car at Caramanga, south of Turin, then shipped to Modena for engines and trimming. Ferrari, Alfa Romeo and Lancia had benefited for some time from being able to dig into Fiat's pockets to finance new and improved models. Now it was Maserati's turn.

Ing. Eugenio Alzati, a thirty-year Fiat veteran who was now managing director of Maserati, was clear where the firm stood in the Fiat hierarchy: above the best Alfa Romeos and Lancias and below the entry-level Ferraris. It was a gap-filler, a small-scale producer of about 2,500 cars a year, which did not shout at people; Maseratis were about good taste without ostentation. His biggest task, he maintained, was to instil in the workforce the concept of increased production with modern quality standards.

'Ranks of fans are waiting for new cars which will be as successful as those which have dominated the racing circuits throughout the world', he declared. 'We cannot and will not disappoint them.'

At this stage, Maserati were selling 40 per cent of output to the domestic Italian market – in some previous years it had been up to 80 per cent – so there was a drive to export more, but not to the USA, of which Fiat were very chary for two reasons. Firstly they maintained that

Who owns Maserati?

In its time Maserati have made not just road and race cars, but also marine engines, machine tools, spark plugs, motor cycles, batteries, electric vans and pick-up trucks. However, no-one called Maserati has had control of the company since 1937.

Alfieri Maserati had begun the company in 1914 in the Via de Pepoli, Bologna with his five *fratelli* (brothers). Their initial business, Societa Anonima Officine Alfieri Maserati, was servicing Isotta Fraschinis and after World War One they developed a sparking plug business, first in Milan and then in the suburbs of Bologna.

Their first complete car was a 1500cc supercharged straight eight, the tipo 26, in which Alfieri was seriously injured in the Coppa Messina in 1927. He died in 1932 at the age of forty-four.

Later cars pioneered the use of magnesium alloy for cylinder heads in 1929 and hydraulic brakes for race cars in 1933. The brothers continued to build notable race cars – with the trident badge changed to an oval in 1930 – until 1939 when they sold out to Adolfo Orsi, an iron and steel magnate from Modena; they agreed to stay on for ten years as consultants.

Orsi moved the company from Bologna to its present Modena home at 322 Viale Ciro Menotti, the avenue named after the city's most famous martyr, hanged in 1831 for his part in the struggle for independence.

The Maserati brothers stayed on under contract as engineers until 1948, but left when Orsi decided to build road cars. The *fratelli* went back to a corner of their old factory in Bologna and founded Officine Specializzate per la Construzione di Automobili Fratelli Maserati, better known as Osca, where they continued development of race cars, building, among others, the Mt4, the most successful racing car in the world under 1500cc.

The original red brick Maserati factory remains at the Viale Ciro Menotti today, alongside the Milan–Bologna railway line, but much has changed since Orsi moved it there to be next to his steel-making business. His son Omar ran the company reasonably successfully – despite a brush with the receiver in 1958 – until he sold out ten years later to Citroën, who wanted the company for its engine expertise.

Citroën used this to produce an engine for their SM sports saloon and built two completely new mid-engined cars, the Bora and the Merak. The early 1970s oil crisis destroyed Maserati's markets and Citroën themselves were failing. They were taken over by Peugeot and Maserati were put into liquidation.

Maserati were rescued in 1973 by the Italian government with the help of Alejandro De Tomaso. Then in 1975, De Tomaso's Benelli motor cycle firm took over most of the shares and in 1989, Fiat Auto bought 49 per cent of Maserati, taking full control four years later.

Fiat is a complicated monster. It is important to distinguish between Fiat Auto (the manufacturer of Fiat, Alfa Romeo and Lancia cars) and the Fiat Group, of which it is a part and in which Maserati and Ferrari presently sit. The Fiat Group also makes Iveco trucks, agricultural and construction machinery and components, and is involved in publications and communications. For instance, it owns Magneti Marelli, the Biturbo's ignition source, and Marelli controls brands such as Carello lighting, Jaeger, Veglia Borletti, Solex and Weber.

continued overleaf

Who owns Maserati? *continued*

The plot thickened in 1997 when Fiat Auto sold Maserati to Ferrari, which in turn was 56 per cent owned by the Fiat Group, with the rest being held mainly by Mediobanca, an Italian bank. It was this deal that led to the huge cash infusion to revive Maserati. (Fiat has subsequently bought back the 29 per cent of the Mediobanco stake, which it sold to them during a financial crisis in 2002.)

In February 2005, Ferrari and Maserati were split up, with Maserati becoming a separate company within the Fiat Group, though Fiat said Maserati would continue to work closely with Ferrari on engine technology and its commercial network. Fiat added that Alfa Romeo and Maserati would establish a close technical and commercial collaboration, especially in big international markets. Alfas are to be sold in the USA through Maserati dealers from 2009.

Evidence of the Fiat 'happy families' game can be seen in the new Alfa Romeo 8C Competizione, whose 4.7-litre V8 engine is an Alfa-modified version of a Maserati engine built by Ferrari, and the car is assembled at the Maserati works in Modena.

Fiat's chief executive, Sergio Marchionne, announced in the summer of 2006 that Maserati would start to make money in 2007, even if it would not be much. Combining Maserati and Alfa Romeo, he said, 'remains one of our objectives'. Maserati sold 5,600 cars in 2005 and lost €35 million in 2006.

Maserati's total production was half that needed to sell the car there cost-effectively. Secondly, there was the legacy of the self-combusting Biturbos and the fear of hugely expensive litigation. 'We will go back to the US when there's legislation to protect the manufacturer as well as the customer', said Alzati, 'you can't spend the company's entire budget in court being sued by a single client.'

Unsold cars

Though owning half the company for several years, Fiat had largely left Maserati to their own devices. In 1992 they had made 983 cars, but still incurred heavy losses. When Alzati arrived, there were 1,000 unsold cars in the pipeline between the factory and the dealerships, some of them more than two model years old. Shifting those cars – effectively a whole year's production – and getting greater reliability from suppliers was his first concern. Improvements to quality cost £4m.

The new Quattroporte had much unseen Fiat input into design and safety features, such as side impact bars in the doors, pre-tensioned seat belts and a progressively deformable bodyshell with crumple zones front and rear. Much was made of the slender, steeply angled windscreen pillars, part of the safety cage in the cabin, and of its performance in crash testing.

It was to have made its debut in December 1993, but was delayed for several months to allow Fiat to develop airbags and an anti-lock braking system.

Despite the Fiat input, the car owed a great deal to its Biturbo-based ancestors: the elegant bodywork was on a stretched version of the 430 floorpan. It was slightly wider and taller than the 430, and had a much bigger boot. Its mechanics had a close relationship with the two cars that appeared with it on the stand at Turin: it was offered with the Shamal's V8 or the 2.8 V6 from the Ghibli. In Italy, there was a 2.0-litre V6 tax-breaker version.

The Shamal's designer, Gandini, had been pressed into service to produce a smaller car than the previous Quattroportes and this new wedge-shaped four door was a logical extension of the 430's four-door theme, rather than being a grand limousine, as this was to be an interim updating – a new product line would need some years to develop.

It was a slippery shape, with a Cd of 0.31, designed to compete with the Jaguar XJR and BMW M5 rather than with the big Mercedes. It cost the same as an S-Class, and was only slightly larger than a Ford Sierra and considerably smaller than its BMW 5 series competitor.

Nevertheless, Maserati's British brochure for the car talked of its impressive size and long wheelbase, combining the distinguishing features of a flagship model with the unmistakeable style of a great sports car. 'The new model is targeted towards an elite clientele', Maserati announced, 'motorists who will go for its exclusive reputation as well as its intrinsic quality in terms of performance, driving pleasure, comfort and luxury.'

High-cut arches

Gandini, who worked on the car with the Maserati Design Centre, incorporated into it his trademark, the high-cut rear wheel arches. 'A typical stroke of Gandini's pencil and one that proves that a substantial shape is no bar to a dashing line', said the brochure.

'It's time Marcello thought of a new trick', commented *Car*. The body shell was built by Pininfarina, painted by Ferrari and completed at Modena where, incidentally, the cars on the production line used to be moved sideways rather than forwards.

It was 14ft 9in (4,550mm) long, compared with its predecessor's 16ft 5in (4,980mm) on a wheelbase of 8ft 6in (2,650mm) – again much smaller than the Quattroporte III's 9ft 2in (2,800mm) – but just as luxurious, with a dashboard in burred elm and leather, eight-way electric seats in Connolly leather from Florence, with a trident embossed into the headrests, automatic air conditioning, central locking, ice warning, and remote opening of the boot and fuel filler cap.

The look of the traditional highly polished elm burr steering wheel was rather spoilt by a huge plastic covering for the driver's airbag (the passenger did without until the Evoluzione). 'As a sophisticated throwback to the past', said the brochure 'the bolts have been left exposed, creating a clever contrast with the airbag.'

There was wood veneer everywhere – even on the windscreen wiper switches. Not everyone was fond of it. 'Do we really need door locks, indicator stalks and air vents covered in the stuff?' asked *Car*.

The first Quattroporte IV iteration, a 2.0-litre for the Italian market, even had the Biturbo V6 engine producing 287bhp at 6,500rpm, with a torque figure of 253lb ft (35kg m) at 3,000rpm; for export there was a 2.8-litre engine producing 284bhp at 6,000rpm and torque of 311lb ft (43kg m) at 3,500rpm. There was the usual twin turbo, twin intercooler installation.

In 1996, a 3.2-litre V8 similar to the Shamal's arrived, but even more powerful at 335bhp at 6,400rpm, which produced an enormous 331.27lb ft (45.8kg m) of torque at 4,400rpm. Maserati claimed that this quad-cam 32-valve engine – castings by Ferrari, machined at Modena – was the most efficient production V8 in the world with a specific output of 104bhp per litre.

It was asserted that this figure of more than 100bhp per litre – for the 2.0-litre and 2.8 V6s and the V8 – could be arrived at because of the low-pressure casting process for the aluminium cylinder heads, which was also used for F1 engines. Top speed of the V8 was nearly 170mph (270km/h) and the 0–62mph (0–100km/h) was 5.7sec according to manufacturer's figures, though contemporary tests put it well beyond 6 seconds.

This was the first Quattroporte since a handful of the first series to be sold with right-hand drive.

Preposterously quick

'It is preposterously quick', reported *Autocar*, 'The leap from 30 to 70mph takes only 5.2sec … the V8 feels and sounds fantastic … it is one of today's most thrilling powerplants.' This 3.2 engine would later power the new-generation 3200 coupé, on which Giugiaro had begun work shortly after the Fiat takeover, and which finally appeared in September 1998.

All the Quattroporte's engines delivered terrific power over 3,000rpm when the twin turbos kicked in. 'It's an enjoyable tool to carry four people at immense speed', said *Car*.

The gearbox was a six-speed Getrag or four-speed ZF automatic; later there was the option of a four-speed BTR automatic gearbox from Australia on the V8, which garnered few good opinions. It was based on an old Borg Warner box and had three modes: normal, with kick-down only when the throttle pedal was on the floor; power, with advanced kick-down when changes happened at higher revs; and ice, for use when there was any. The ice mode was engaged automatically by temperature and oil pressure sensors. At the back was a limited-slip differential (later a ZF) with a 3.25:1 ratio for the manual and 3.90:1 for the auto.

Brakes were self-ventilating, cross-drilled discs with Brembo four-pot floating calipers and, at last, Bosch ABS. On the V6, tyres were 205/45ZR × 16 front and 225/45ZR × 16 rear; 17in rims were available as an option and were standard on the V8.

Suspension was, like the Shamal, four-way electronically adjustable on the V8 as standard, but a £1,500 extra on the V6. The rear featured a welded tubular lattice structure, adjustable for camber, as used by the Ghiblis in the Open Cup championship. There were six body colours offered, two greens, two blues, grey and red.

The Quattroporte was at last available in right-hand drive. Prices in the UK at the end of 1997 were: manual Quattroporte V6 £49,995; V8 manual £57,995; and automatic transmission was £1,800 extra. *Sports Car International*, who tested an early 2.0-litre version, reported:

> It's a nicely cut Armani suit of a car, that combines traditional Maserati virtues like lively, enjoyable handling and an engaging, powerful driveline with a well-honed and dignified package for the occupants. Its only disappointments are a trace of imprecision in hard steering maneuvers (sic) some silly oversights by the interior design team and an excess of engine noise over 4,000rpm.

When the 2.8-litre version arrived in Britain, it cost £56,910, the price of 1½ BMW M3s; the Jaguar XJR was £10,000 cheaper. Maserati's chief executive, Ing. Alzati, was quoted as saying, 'Our cars were too cheap – that is why we have increased prices over the past two years and that is why demand is increasing.' Discuss this proposition and its place in the real world.

Complete Car tested the 2.8 in 1996, giving it three stars, compared with five for the M3 and four for the XJR. On the plus side were exclusivity, performance and brakes; on the minus were high price (though it admitted that only a philistine would judge a Maserati on value-for-money), mediocre quality and weak traction. In the wet they had found that this combined with turbo boost led to vicious tail-whipping – so not much had changed since the Biturbo's early days:

> Buying a Quattroporte is all about obtaining a part of Italian culture and a small slice of motoring history. You get a sporting saloon that in one respect drives all its competitors into oblivion – and that's exclusiveness.

The Evoluzione

In July 1997, Fiat passed day-to-day control of Maserati to Ferrari, who closed the factory at Viale Ciro Menotti at the end of that year for extensive refurbishment. The mayor of Modena had offered Maserati a new site for the rebirth – the deserted Bugatti factory at Campogaliano, built for the ill-fated EB 110 – but it was rejected as it was felt that Viale Ciro Menotti was Maserati's historic home.

When the factory re-opened some four months later, with Luca di Montezemolo as managing director, the Quattroporte went into production again and emerged in March 1998, looking very much the same, but badged as the Quattroporte Evoluzione, available with the V8 and V6 engines.

However, Fiat maintained that 800 components had been improved and more than 400

Quattroporte IV (1994–2001)

2.0 V6 engine

Type	AM573
Layout	V6 90 degrees – 4 valves per cylinder, double overhead cam per bank, two IHI turbo-chargers
Bore × stroke:	82 × 63mm
Capacity:	1996cc
Compression ratio:	7.6:1
Max power:	287bhp/214kW@6,500rpm
Max torque:	253lb ft/35kg m@3,000rpm
Fuel system:	Weber Marelli injection
Intercoolers:	2

2.8 V6 engine

Type	AM574
Layout	V6 90 degrees – 4 valves per cylinder, double overhead cam per bank, two IHI turbo-chargers
Bore × stroke:	94 × 67mm
Capacity:	2790cc
Compression ratio:	7.4:1
Max power:	284bhp/211kW@6,000rpm
Max torque:	311lb ft/43kg m@3,000rpm
Fuel system:	Weber Marelli injection
Intercoolers:	2

3.2 V8 engine

Type	AM578
Layout	V8 90 degrees – 2 valves per cylinder, double overhead cam per bank, two IHI roller-bearing turbochargers
Bore × stroke:	80 × 80mm
Capacity:	3217cc
Compression ratio:	7.3:1
Max power:	335bhp/249kW@6,400rpm
Max torque:	331lb ft/45.8kg m@3,000rpm
Fuel system:	Weber Marelli injection
Intercoolers:	2

Transmission

Gearbox:	Getrag manual 6-speed; automatic ZF 4-speed (V6); BTR 4-speed (V8)
Final drive:	ZF 3.45:1; 3.25:1 (2.8)

Suspension

Front:	Independent, four-position electronic adjustment
Steering:	Variable resistance power-assisted rack and pinion with double gearing servo
Brakes:	Double circuit servo-assisted

Running gear

Wheels:	V6: 7J × 16; V8: 8J × 17 (opt) 9in (Evo)
Tyres:	V6: 205/55 ZR16 (front) V8: 225/45 ZR17 (front) V6: 225/55 ZR16 (rear) V8: 245/40 ZR17 (rear)

Performance

Max speed:	V6: 162mph (260km/h) V8: 168mph (270km/h)
Acceleration:	0-62mph (120km/h): V6: 5.9secs; V8: 5.8sec

Dimensions

Wheelbase:	104.3in (2,650mm)
Front track:	59.9in (1,522mm)
Rear track:	59.1in (1,502mm)
Length:	179.1in (4,550mm)
Width:	71.3in (1,810mm)
Height:	54.3in (1,380mm)
Weight:	3,402lb (1,543kg) (manual) 3,632lb (1,647kg)

Number built 2,400

had been changed. *Top Gear* suggested that the 401st change should be to firm up the steering and improve cornering feedback and the 402nd to beef up the air con. However, it added, there had been substantial improvements over the previous model, though there was still too much wood and Alcantara.

'The heart of a racing car, the comfort of a prestigious saloon, the style of a car with distinctive lines', trumpeted the brochure, which in a curious throwback, extolled the virtues of the original engine used in the Merak between 1975 and 1983 as the starting point of what it called this latest generation ofV6 engines.

Outwardly, on the larger-engined car, the only sign of change were the V8 Evoluzione badges on the front wings, replacing the *ottocilindri* script on the later version of the Quattroporte. It was, however, a much better-built car, constructed to Ferrari standards. 'The list of downsides is now much shorter than before', said *Car* magazine.

The famous Lasalle clock disappeared – the management said it reminded them too much of the previous era; yet another managing director of Maserati, this time Paolo Marinsek, said it was a 'signature of the De Tomaso period', which they were trying to put behind them. In its place was a cheap quartz digital clock near the gear lever, which was very difficult to see. There was a different steering wheel and dashboard, and changes to the interior trim, with darker wood being used.

The brochure talked of new 16in eight-spoke alloys, with 17in alloys as an option. Basic mechanics were the same as previously, though unseen changes were made to the cylinder head and crankshaft, and there were modifications to the wiring harness, clutch and cooling systems. It came in fourteen body colours rather than the original six.

Car reported in July 1998: 'Sumptuous and extravagant materials abound. Alcantara dresses the ceiling, the facia, the instrument binnacle hood, parts of the doors and pretty much anything else that isn't surfaced in wood and leather.'

The Quattroporte had a belter of an engine: 'The turbos spool up with astonishing ease, giving you the grunt of a field full of pigs at almost any speed and almost any gear.'

The Ferrari influence had led to a far more convincing feel of solidity, and an awful lot of the raw edges had been burnished off. The price in Britain in September 1998 was £58,795 for the V8.

'You'd be much better off with a Mercedes, a Jaguar or a BMW', said *Car*. 'They are more modern, more capable and equipped with state-of-the-art systems. Yet they are nowhere near as exclusive and, with the possible exception of the XJR, not half as much fun as the Italian car.' *Autocar* commented: 'Getting rid of the old-style clock is one thing, but not even Ferrari can eradicate the De Tomaso influence from the basic engineering … (it) benefits enormously from this makeover, but it's never going to be a great car.'

Production of the Evoluzione version ended on 27 March 2001, after 782 cars. The total number produced of Quattroporte IVs and the Evo was 2,375.

Because of the Maserati reputation for fierce depreciation, Andrea Zappia, the sales director, was quoted in 1998 as saying that the company was considering offering guaranteed buy-back prices. Little more was heard of this ambitious plan. However, it is worth noting that the new Quattroporte, according to a 2006 survey of the Italian market by *Sanguinetti Editore*, was the highest-rated car for retaining its value in the G luxury sector, after the Ferrari F430.

Since its international launch in September 2003, the Maserati Quattroporte had received by February 2006 a total of twenty-seven international awards and spearheaded Maserati's remarkable recovery. In 2005, 3,500 Quattroportes were sold worldwide, 1,550 of them in North America.

16 Buying and restoration – the Biturbo range

The two main enemies are rust and crash damage, the latter perhaps more common than in other classic cars because the Biturbo can be wayward in its handling. Andy Heywood at the Maserati specialists Bill McGrath says that of the cars he sees, he would recommend not more than one in ten, up to the end of the 222 generation.

Unseen rust is a particular problem with the car's bulkhead, which allows water into the footwells and fusebox. 'You can't really do a 100 per cent repair unless you take the car to pieces', says Andy Heywood. 'In the future people may do that, but at the moment they are not.'

Rust can also get into sills and into the suspension mountings at the front. It is also worth checking the usual rot spots as in on all cars: the wings, boot floors, the edges of doors and the bottom of pillars.

The majority of electrical problems stem from the fact that the fuse box from the Fiat Strada is of poor quality, causing all sorts of intermittent electrical faults, ranging from irregular running and dim lights to failing to start at all. Canny owners often put things right for a while by kicking the footwell or slamming the glovebox lid. A fusebox repair service based in Allen, Texas, for a fixed price

Not for the faint-hearted … restoration begins on an early carburetted Biturbo. (Mike Roberts)

Taking the head off an engine that has not run for some time can produce a nasty surprise – like these pistons rusted in their liners. (Dan McCallum)

A Biturbo SE undergoes a comprehensive overhaul. This one-owner-from-new car has Momo wheels.

The Maserati is a complex beast, requiring many special tools to maintain.

of $59.99 is sometimes advertised on eBay.

The fused relays for lots of different functions like headlamps and air conditioning were also badly designed. Failure of the relay to the fan can cause the engine to overheat and blow a head gasket. Much more reliable relays are now available. The first 65-amp alternators were upgraded to a more reliable 105-amp version. The basic wiring itself causes no difficulties. The speedometer, which works from a low-voltage electrical sensor, can be unpredictable and fail.

Interior trim is reasonably robust for an 1980s car. The door panels tend to fall to pieces because they are made in about four different parts and screwed together: over the years everything gets loose. The seats are very good; the original cord interior is better than the first leather interiors, particularly in the Biturbo II, which tend to dry out and crack very badly in hot climates. Dashboards and the backs of seats seem particularly affected. In the 222 and 430 there were Alcantara side bolsters that tend to wear out prematurely; they are difficult to replace to make them look original.

Vital oil changes

For the engine's good health, regular oil changes are vital – at least every 6,000 miles (10,000km) if not sooner. This prolongs turbo life enormously. So does letting the engine idle for a while after a run. Some owners adopt the two-minute rule – warm up for at least two minutes, avoid short trips and idle for another two minutes before turning the engine off.

The likelihood of turbo failure in carburetted cars can be checked by disconnecting the high-pressure hose from the turbos to the plenum chamber and checking inside – oil there is a bad sign. Replacement turbos are widely available and not unduly costly, but the roller bearing turbos in the Ghibli Cup cars and in the Quattroporte Evoluzione are wildly expensive.

Alloy wheel corrosion is common, as damp gets beneath the lacquer. The only solution is to have the wheels expensively refurbished.

Cracked exhaust manifolds are common; this is a problem often caused by the engine being switched off when the turbos are still very hot. The heat sink as the car is cooling leads to differential contraction rates, which cause the fracture.

All early cars should have had the small gauze filter removed from the oil gallery in the cylinder head, as it clogs, leaving cams short of oil and prone to seize. The engines have to have regular cam belt changes – every 24,000 miles (39,000km) or four years. Wear in the crankshaft bearings can lead to a drop in oil pressure, starving the camshafts of lubricant and causing them to seize in their housings, with predictable and dire results.

On the four-valve engine, which has four camshafts, only one in each bank is driven by the belt at the front of the engine. The inlet cams are driven by small chains at the back of each side of the engine, which have to be renewed every 48,000 miles (75,000km) or so. If this is done properly, the engine has to be removed – a major job, taking about thirty hours or so, and thus very expensive. However, not doing it would be even more so if, as is likely, the pistons and valves have a fatal meeting. This engine-out job affects all the four-valve cars up to the last Ghiblis and V6 Quattroportes.

Some later cars like the Ghibli could be fitted with electronic shock absorbers, but Andy Heywood says they are not particularly reliable. Problems with leaks or seized motors are common, and they are very expensive to replace.

On starting the engine, oil pressure should rise to 5 bar and stay there whatever the speed. Hot idle will cause the pressure to drop, but it should never be less than half on the gauge (2.5 bar).

Strong bottom end

The bottom end of the engine is very strong and was unchanged from the start of Biturbo production up to and including the Ghibli, which, given the huge increase in power over the years, is quite an achievement. Maserati do not supply oversize bearings as they assume that the crankshaft will never need to be ground. Indeed, Bill McGrath have rebuilt a 160,000-mile engine and put back the original crank.

As to the cooling system, regular changes of anti-freeze are needed, as the cars can suffer from corrosion. And with the myriad of pipes – far more than most cars because of the turbos – regular checks are advisable.

One of the recurrent complaints about the turbo boost gauge was its lack of calibration. Basically, everything is OK if the needle gets into the yellow segment at 5,000rpm or so. At low speed or on the overrun, it can be below that. Beware if it hits the red, or if the car has been modified to squeeze out more boost.

Customized panels for Ghiblis and other Maseratis are offered by Carrozzeria Campana in Modena.

The suspension is the least troublesome of any of the major mechanical components, as it is mostly fairly basic. But on very early cars the rear subframe could suffer stress cracks and corrode; this was rectified by the Biturbo II. The trailing arms could get bent quite easily and rot at the shock absorber mountings. The front shock absorbers were wont to leak.

In the transmission, breather holes blocked very easily in early cars leading to undue pressure, which blew the oil seals, but most of these will now have been fitted quickly and easily with a larger breather. But whine can denote a failing differential.

There was also an endemic problem with clonking in the drive train – which appeared again in the 3200. Spyders and Karifs suffer in particular with a transmission knock and vibration at low speed. The vibration can come from misalignment of the centre prop-shaft bearing, the knock from the differential itself.

Brian Cherrington, who was at GKN at the time it supplied the Biturbo units, says it was due to the large number of gear meshes in both the Sensitork and the Ranger units. The solution, outlined a factory service bulletin, was to use Loctite to knit together the cone and splines in the differential. All units need checking for oil loss, which can lead to overheating.

Andy Heywood estimates the cost of an engine overhaul for cars of the Biturbo era at about £5,000 at 2005 prices, including new pistons and liners, valves, belts, seals, bearings and gaskets. The cost of a body rebuild is about the same.

Reasonable prices

Parts are surprisingly accessible – almost anything for a 1986 Biturbo is available and prices are reasonable, though they go up for the Ghibli era. But when specific parts run out, they can take some time to be re-commissioned. New BITURBO chrome script badges are available (from www.abarthbadges.com).

Finally, check the obvious – service records to see whether timing belts/chains have been replaced. Do all the electrical gadgets, particularly the electric windows, work? And, of course, check whether the engine runs – this new owner in December 2005 had a nasty surprise which he reported on the Maserati bulletin board:

> Hi All,
>
> I just bought a Biturbo on eBay and find no carburettor under the cover. HELP ... Need a new or used carb.

Running on unleaded

Unleaded fuel was not around at the time of the early Biturbos. When unleaded arrived, the factory recommended an upgrade for early cars to modified cylinder heads with hardened valve seats, though it's far cheaper to use additives than to convert the heads. American cars were

Enough to make the purists blanch ... Mutany Automotive in Oxfordshire offer glass fibre body customizing kits for the Ghibli. This example is painted in House of Kolor sunrise pearl yellow, topped with a clear show lacquer. (David McCalium)

Chassis decoder

Chassis numbers on early cars can be found on the bulkhead; later cars have them on the slam panel above the radiator.

Although most people call them chassis numbers, since October 1979 they have been known officially as VIN numbers, a seventeen-character unique identifier for every vehicle produced in the world. The system was defined originally by the International Organization for Standardization (ISO).

Country of origin

The first three characters or so identify the country and manufacturer of origin and are known as the WMI, the World Manufacturer Identifier (WMI). The world is split into six continents, with European manufacturers using the last eight letters of the alphabet, though these bear no relation to their own initial letters.

So, for example, a car made in the United Kingdom is identified by a sequence between SA-SM, France between VF-VR and the Italians between ZA-ZR. They are almost bottom of the pile in the listings, just ahead these days of Slovenia.

So what does ZAM331BOOGB180004 mean? An Italian Maserati Biturbo coupé, made in 1986 in Milan, right-hand drive, car number 004.

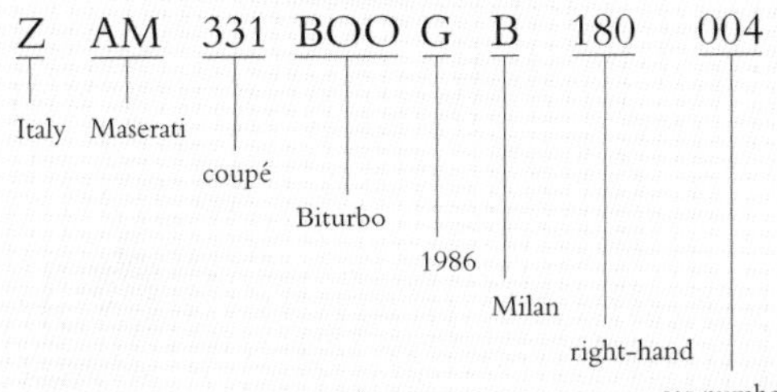

One of the very first cars destined for the UK, with the chassis plate on the bulkhead. It is in fact the fourth right-hand-drive coupé to be built. It still exists, though is probably beyond repair.

The maker

The second set of letters denotes the car maker – Maserati is ZAM (Alfieri Maserati), Fiat is ZFA, Ferrari ZFF, etc.

The type defined by number

331	Two-door coupé	336	Ghibli
332	425/430	337	Quattroporte IV
333	Spyder 2.5/2.8	338	3200GT
333	Karif	339	Shamal
334	228		

The model year

D = 1982/3	H = 1987	M = 1991
E = 1984	J = 1988	N = 1992
F = 1985	K = 1989	P = 1993
G = 1986	L = 1990	R = 1994

continued overleaf

This plate denotes that the car is a right-hand-drive Spyder, built in Modena in 1987. The version plate shows it is a 2.5.

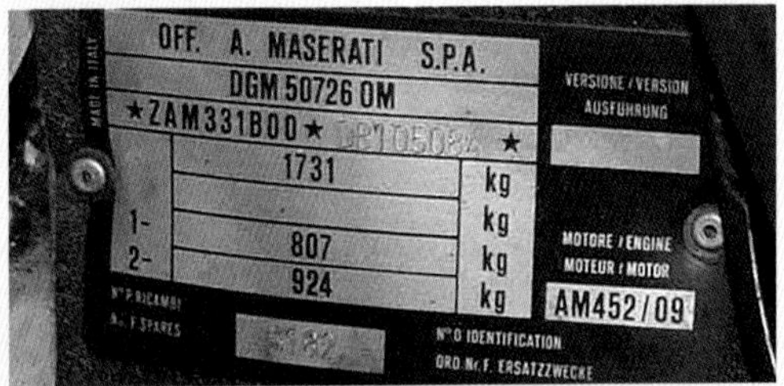

All cars had the chassis number stamped into the bodywork as well as being displayed on a bulkhead panel. The is the eighty-fourth Biturbo coupé to be built.

Chassis decoder *continued*

After 1994, the date figures were largely replaced with two zeros. So ZAM336BOO 00400114 was a right-hand drive Ghibli with ABS.

The place of manufacture

A = Modena
B = Lambrate, Milan
All 228s and Karifs were built in Modena, as were a proportion of Spyders that were not built at Zagato. After 1994, all cars were made in Modena as Fiat closed the Lambrate factory in Milan and the year letter from then on was replaced with 00.

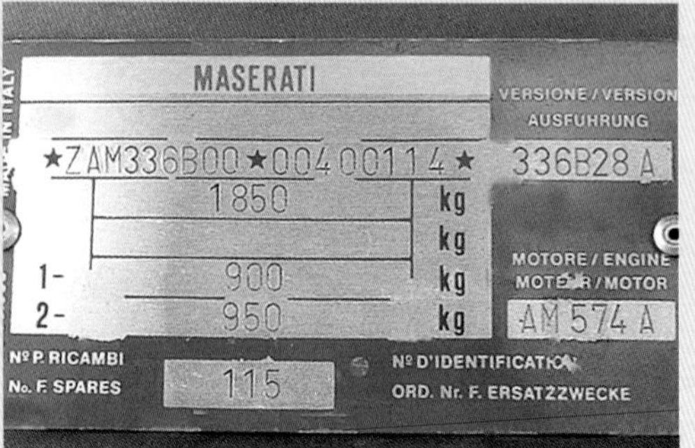

In the last four years of production, the letters for year and place of manufacture were replaced with zeros. This is on a 2.8 Ghibli.

Right-hand drive

This is signified by:

180 for coupés, other than the 228, which was 190. This figure of 190 was also used for the Spyder and Karif. Four-door cars were 290. Left-hand drive cars used a different series of numbers.

fitted with catalysers from the outset, so are not affected.

For other markets these were the recommendations in a factory bulletin of November 1999:

- V6 engines of 2000 and 2500cc with the three-valve head produced after 26 March 1987 can use unleaded. The change was made at unit 15,046.
- V6 engines of 2000cc with the four-valve head are suitable for unleaded from unit 803,326, produced on 16 January 1992. The heads are marked with an S or 490.
- V6 engines of 2800cc with both three- and four-valve heads can be used with unleaded fuel.
- V8 engines of 3200cc are also suitable for unleaded.

The customized Ghibli engine has twin racing air filters and can run on injected nitrous oxide from a single large bottle in the boot. It is set up so that the driver can manually inject the nitrous oxide only when the throttle is fully open. (David McCalium)

Useful contacts

Specialists UK

Bill McGrath Maserati

Bill McGrath Maserati started out with the eponymous Bill as a one-man band working in a barn in the early 1970s. His restoration of his own 3500GT won him many Maserati customers and he formed his company in 1976.

In 1984, he moved to the present site at Kimpton, Hertfordshire, and two years later he became a dealer for the new Biturbo range – despite having no showroom – because the directors of Maserati UK were so impressed with his work.

When Maserati UK failed in 1990 and Meridien took over the concession, the company became an official service agent. By that time the general manager was Andy Heywood, who has owned the company since 2004. Its status since the Ferrari takeover is that of official independent Maserati specialist.

Bill McGrath has a staff of ten and handles everything from routine servicing to complete restoration. The Biturbo expert is Paul Molyneaux, who has been with the company since 1991.
Unit 8 Claggy Road, Kimpton
Herts, SG4 8QB
Tel +44 (0)1438 832 161
www.classicmaseratis.co.uk

Autoshield

Based in Manchester, Autoshield is run by Marios Kriticos who says he has been in operation since 1985, becoming an official Maserati service dealer in 1989. It offers a complete restoration service and an extensive range of parts.
322c & 465 Barlow Moor Road
Chorlton-cum-Hardy
Manchester, M21 8AU
Tel/fax +44 (0) 161 881 3463

Meridien Modena

Meridien was once the sole importer of Maseratis in the UK and still retains the Maserati dealership for the south coast.
77 High Street, Lyndhurst,
Hampshire, SO43 7PB
Tel: + 44 (0) 2380 283404
www.modena.meridien.co.uk

Specialists USA

MIE Corporation

MIE Corp. is the commercial arm of the Maserati Club International in the USA, sharing a 30,000sq ft facility with the club in Auburn, Washington, a suburb of Seattle. In December 1994, MIE bought the complete stock of spare parts of the US Maserati distributor and claims to be the world's largest independent distributor of new and used classic Maserati spare parts and accessories. The club side, Maserati Club International, publish the magazine *VIALE CIRO MENOTTI.*
1620 Industry Drive SW, Suite F
Auburn, WA 98001, USA
Tel + 253-833-2598; www.maseratinet.com

Specialists Italy

Two very well-known firms across the street from each other in Modena who have worked with Maserati for years:

Giuseppe Candini

Legendary restorer of Maseratis. From 1953 to 1958 Giuseppe Candini was with Maserati's race support team where he worked with many top racing drivers.
Via Tito Livio, 19
41100 Modena, Italy
Tel: 059/828280
www.modenaweb.com/candini

Carrozzeria Campana

This firm bought from Maserati the entire stock of parts for cars from 1959–82, and also do bodywork and restoration.
Via Tito Livio, 60
41100 Modena, Italy
Tel: 059/828079
www.campanacarrozzeria.it

Other specialists

Details of all other Maserati dealers world-wide can be found at www.maserati.com

Clubs

The Maserati Club UK

The Maserati Club UK was founded in 1972 and provides information, assistance with ownership and a programme of events in the United Kingdom and abroad. It produces a regular newsletter and a first-class glossy magazine, *Trident*.
Maserati Club
2 Sunny Bank, Widmer End
Buckinghamshire, HP15 6PA
Tel/Fax: +44 (0) 1494 717 701
www.maseraticlub.co.uk

The Maserati Club (TMC)

This club has four US and seven international TMC chapters:
Eastern Chapter (based in New York)
Southeast Chapter (based in Florida)
Rocky Mountain Chapter (based in Colorado)
California Chapter (based in California)
TMC: Canada (based in Toronto, Canada)
Maserati Club of Japan (based in Tokyo, Japan)
Club Maserati Australia (based in Sydney, Australia)
TMC: South Africa (based in Rivonia, South Africa)
TMC: Scuderia del Tridente (based in Venice, Italy)
TMC: Hungary (based in Budapest, Hungary)
TMC: Global (based in New Jersey, USA)
The club magazine is *iL TRIDENTE*.

Main contact (in USA):
TMC
PO Box 5300
Somerset, NJ 08875-5300, USA
Tel: +001 732 249 2177
email@themaseraticlub.com

The Maserati Club of Australia, Inc.

This club was founded in 1981. It is based in Melbourne.
PO Box 6058
Cromer, VIC 3193, Australia
Tel: + 61 3 9515
www.maserati.org.au

BiturboClubItalia

BiturboClubItalia
Via Sostegno 8
10146 Torino, Italy
Tel: 011 726024
www.biturboclubitalia.it

Other clubs worldwide

Maserati Club Holland
www.maseraticlub.nl

Maserati Club of Germany
www.deutschermaseraticlub.de

Maserati Classico Belgium
www.maseraticlassico.be

Chrysler TC by Maserati
www.chryslertcbymaseraticlub.com

Bibliography

Clarke, R.M. (ed.), *Maserati Performance Portfolio* (Brooklands Books, UK, undated)

Cucchi, Antello, *Maserati: Catalogue Raisoneé* (Automobili, Milan, 1990)

Cucchi, Antello, *New Maseratis* (Automobili, Milan, 1989)

Gonelli, Enio, *Maserati nel Terzo Millennio* (Artestampa, Modena, 2001)

Levin, Doron P., *Behind the wheel at Chrysler* (Harcourt Brace, New York, 1955)

Marchianò, Michele, *Zagato, seventy years in the fast lane* (Giorgo Nada Editore, Milan, 1989)

Qvale, Kjell, *I never looked back* (Privately published, USA, 2005)

Tabucchi, Maurizio, *Maserati, grand prix, sports and GT* (Giorgo Nada Editore, Milan, 2003)

Unique Motor Books, *Maserati 1931–2003 road tests* (Unique Motor Books, UK, 2005)

Wyss, Wallace A., *De Tomaso automobiles* (Osprey, London, 1981)

Periodicals: *Autocar, Auto Italia, Car, Fast Lane, Motor, Motor Sport, Performance Car, Road & Track, Sports Car International, Trident, iL* (sic) *TRIDENTE*

Web resources

www.maserati-indy.co.uk/alfieri00a.htm: Enrico's Maserati pages. A vast range of information on Maserati matters, regularly updated and a selection of excellent pictures. Very useful.

www.maserati-rc.org: Maserati Resource Centre. Does what it says – provides a parts interchange database and technical stuff, plus lots more. Put together by George Perfect in England.

www.maseratilife.com: Maserati Life – forums and cars for sale.

www.home.att.net/~mabc/: Biturbo Central – facts and figures.

http://autos.groups.yahoo.com/group/biturbozentrum: discussion group.

http://autos.groups.yahoo.com/group/maseratibiturbozentrum: discussion group.

www.repartocorse.net/eindex.htm: Reparto Corso – an Italian help forum.

www.maseratisti.net: Maseratisti – community site.

Index

Alfieri, Giulio 12, 29
Alzati, Eugenio 42, 139, 158, 162

Bertocchi, Aurelio 106
Bertocchi, Guarino 14, 29, 32, 76
Briant, Dr David 74

Campana Carozzeria 155, 174
Candini, Guiseppe 174
Casarini, Giordano 12, 19, 21, 27, 34, 35, 37
Cazalet, Anthony 12, 41, 55, 58, 62, 143
Chrysler TC 65–74
Citroën 9, 10, 29, 159
Crane, Scot 153
Cunningham, Brian 86

Dauch, Dick 72
De Tomaso, Alejandro 6–13, 17–18, 35, 39, 43, 53, 58, 60–2, 65, 67, 70, 91, 122, 127–8, 159
Duggleby, John 94

Edmiston, Robert 60–2
Embo 91

Ferrari 6, 154, 160, 162, 164
Fiat 26, 138, 159–60, 162

Gandini, Marcello 130, 142, 161
Garbutt, George 12, 21
Giugiaro, Giorgetto 123
Golden Car 158

Heywood, Andy 8, 165, 169

Iacocca, Lee 65, 67, 69, 72
Innocenti 10, 13, 15, 123, 158
Ital Design 123

Kacher, George 131, 135

Lasalle 56, 164

Maraffi, Luigi 62
Maserati, Alfieri 159
Maserati models:
- 222 101
- 222E 102, 105
- 222SE 105–6
- 222SR 112
- 222 4v 112
- 2.24v 107
- 228 81–88
- 4.18v 63
- 420–425 53–9, 63
- 4.24v 80
- 430 75–9
- Barchetta 143
- Biturbo I and II 6, 14, 17–26, 27–38
- Biturbo 2.5 39–42
- Biturbo E 46
- Biturbo i 48
- Biturbo S 47–8
- Biturbo SE 50
- Chubasco 142
- Ghibli 138–55
  - Cup 145–51
  - GT 142
  - KS 97
  - MY94 141
  - MY95 141
  - Open Cup 143–4
  - Primatist 153–4
- Karif 115–20
- Quattroporte 53
  - I–III 121–6
  - IV 157–62
  - Evoluzione 162
  - Royale 124
- Spyder 89–100

May, Nick 41, 62
McGrath, Bill 47, 94, 165, 173
Meridian Modena 63, 173
Missoni 44

OPAC 98
Orsi, Adolfo, 144

Perinin, Giancarlo 85, 140

Quaife 76–7
Qvale, Kjell 60

Tozzi-Condivi, Mario 60–2

Van der Weele, J. 98
Verganti, Francesco 45

Zagato 89, 91, 92